1 MONTH OF
FREE
READING

at

www.ForgottenBooks.com

By purchasing this book you are eligible for one month membership to ForgottenBooks.com, giving you unlimited access to our entire collection of over 1,000,000 titles via our web site and mobile apps.

To claim your free month visit:

www.forgottenbooks.com/free909744

ISBN 978-0-266-91933-9
PIBN 10909744

This book is a reproduction of an important historical work. Forgotten Books uses
state-of-the-art technology to digitally reconstruct the work, preserving the original format
whilst repairing imperfections present in the aged copy. In rare cases, an imperfection in
the original, such as a blemish or missing page, may be replicated in our edition. We do,
however, repair the vast majority of imperfections successfully; any imperfections that
remain are intentionally left to preserve the state of such historical works.

BLUFFTON COLLEGE
THE ANNUAL CATALOG
FOR 1918-19

BLUFFTON, OHIO

CALENDAR

1918

May 24—Friday—Final examinations for the Second Semester begin.

May 26—Sunday—Baccalaureate Service.

May 29—Wednesday—Class Day.

May 30—Thursday—Alumni Day.
Annual Meeting of the Board of Trustees.

May 31—Friday—Eighteenth Annual Commencement.

June 3—Monday—Summer School begins.

July 4—Thursday—A holiday.

Aug. 16—Friday—Summer School ends.

Sept. 10—Tuesday—Entrance Examinations and Registration.

Sept. 11—Wednesday—The First Semester begins.

Nov. 28—Thursday—A holiday.

Dec. 20—Friday—Christmas recess begins.

1919

Jan. 1.—Wednesday—Christmas recess ends.

Jan. 18—Saturday—Final Examinations for the First Semester begin.

Jan. 22—Wednesday—Final Examinations for the First Semester end.

Jan. 23—Thursday—Registration Day.

Jan. 24—Friday—Second Semester begins.

Feb. 22—Saturday—A holiday.

April 18—Friday—Easter Recess begins.

April 22—Tuesday—Easter Recess ends.

May 23—Friday—Final Examinations for the Second Semester begin.

May 25—Sunday—Baccalaureate Service.

May 28—Wednesday—Class Day.

May 29—Thursday—Alumni Day.

May 30—Friday—Nineteenth Annual Commencement.

June 2—Monday—Summer School begins.

CALENDAR 1918

APRIL						
S	M	T	W	T	F	S
..	1	2	3	4	5	6
7	8	9	10	11	12	13
14	15	16	17	18	19	20
21	22	23	24	25	26	27
28	29	30	..	..	..	..

MAY						
S	M	T	W	T	F	S
..	..	..	1	2	3	4
5	6	7	8	9	10	11
12	13	14	15	16	17	18
19	20	21	22	23	24	25
26	27	28	29	30	31	..

JUNE						
S	M	T	W	T	F	S
..	..	..	..	..	..	1
2	3	4	5	6	7	8
9	10	11	12	13	14	15
16	17	18	19	20	21	22
23	24	25	26	27	28	29
30	..	..	..	..	..	..

JULY						
S	M	T	W	T	F	S
..	1	2	3	4	5	6
7	8	9	10	11	12	13
14	15	16	17	18	19	20
21	22	23	24	25	26	27
28	29	30	31	..	..	..

AUGUST						
S	M	T	W	T	F	S
..	..	..	..	1	2	3
4	5	6	7	8	9	10
11	12	13	14	15	16	17
18	19	20	21	22	23	24
25	26	27	28	29	30	31

SEPTEMBER						
S	M	T	W	T	F	S
1	2	3	4	5	6	7
8	9	10	11	12	13	14
15	16	17	18	19	20	21
22	23	24	25	26	27	28
29	30	..	..	..	..	..

OCTOBER						
S	M	T	W	T	F	S
..	..	1	2	3	4	5
6	7	8	9	10	11	12
13	14	15	16	17	18	19
20	21	22	23	24	25	26
27	28	29	30	31	..	..

NOVEMBER						
S	M	T	W	T	F	S
..	..	..	..	..	1	2
3	4	5	6	7	8	9
10	11	12	13	14	15	16
17	18	19	20	21	22	23
24	25	26	27	28	29	30

DECEMBER						
S	M	T	W	T	F	S
1	2	3	4	5	6	7
8	9	10	11	12	13	14
15	16	17	18	19	20	21
22	23	24	25	26	27	28
29	30	31	..	..	..	..

CALENDAR 1919

JANUARY						
S	M	T	W	T	F	S
..	..	..	1	2	3	4
5	6	7	8	9	10	11
12	13	14	15	16	17	18
19	20	21	22	23	24	25
26	27	28	29	30	31	..

FEBRUARY						
S	M	T	W	T	F	S
..	..	..	..	..	..	1
2	3	4	5	6	7	8
9	10	11	12	13	14	15
16	17	18	19	20	21	22
23	24	25	26	27	28	..

MARCH						
S	M	T	W	T	F	S
..	..	..	..	..	..	1
2	3	4	5	6	7	8
9	10	11	12	13	14	15
16	17	18	19	20	21	22
23	24	25	26	27	28	29
30	31	..	..	..	..	..

APRIL						
S	M	T	W	T	F	S
..	..	1	2	3	4	5
6	7	8	9	10	11	12
13	14	15	16	17	18	19
20	21	22	23	24	25	26
27	28	29	30	..	..	..

MAY						
S	M	T	W	T	F	S
..	..	..	..	1	2	3
4	5	6	7	8	9	10
11	12	13	14	15	16	17
18	19	20	21	22	23	24
25	26	27	28	29	30	31

JUNE						
S	M	T	W	T	F	S
1	2	3	4	5	6	7
8	9	10	11	12	13	14
15	16	17	18	19	20	21
22	23	24	25	26	27	28
29	30	..	..	..	..	..

TRUSTEES, OFFICERS, FACULTY AND COMMITTEES

OFFICERS OF ADMINISTRATION

SAMUEL K. MOSIMAN, President.

NOAH E. BYERS, Dean of College.

JACOB H. LANGENWALTER, Dean of Seminary.

EDITH McPEAKE, Dean of Women.

GUSTAV A. LEHMANN, Dean of Conservatory.

C. HENRY SMITH, Secretary.

JOHN R. THIERSTEIN, Acting Treasurer and Business Manager.

EDMUND J. HIRSCHLER, Registrar.

WILLIAM G. EGLY, Librarian.

BOYD D. SMUCKER, Field Secretary.

FLOYD PANNEBECKER, Assistant Librarian.

MRS. LOUISE YODER, Matron of Ropp Hall.

ETHEL STEINMAN, Secretary to the President.

ABRAM RICKERT, Assistant Bookkeeper.

ELMER LEHMAN, Engineer.

C. D. AMSTUTZ, Superintendent of Grounds.

THE FACULTY

REV. SAMUEL K. MOSIMAN, Ph. D., President; Professor of Old Testament Language and Literature.

A. B., Wittenberg College, 1897; Superintendent of Mennonite Mission School, Cantonment, Okla., 1897-1902; B. D., McCormick Seminary, 1905; Nettie F. McCormick Hebrew Scholar, 1905-07; Ph. D., University of Halle, Germany, 1907; Teacher of Greek and Philosophy, Lebanon College, 1908; Professor of Greek and Old Testament Language and Literature, Bluffton College, 1908-09; President, Bluffton College, 1909—.

EDMUND JOHN HIRSCHLER, S. M., Professor of Mathematics and Astronomy.

A. B., University of Kansas, 1901; Phi Beta Kappa, 1901; Sigma Xi, 1901; Instructor in German, Rose Polytechnic Institute, 1901-03; Graduate student in Department of Mathematics, The University of Chicago, Summers of 1914, 1915 and 1916; S. M., The University of Chicago, 1916; Professor of Mathematics and Astronomy, Bluffton College, 1903—.

HAROLD B. ADAMS, Professor of Pianoforte and Organ.

Student of Morris, Amy Fay, Sherwood, Godowsky; Instructor in Piano, Holton, Kans., 1884-85; Berea College, 1885-89; Heidelberg University, 1886-96; Lima College, 1896-1907; Organist at St. Paul's Lutheran Church, Lima, O., 1900-1913; Professor of Pianoforte, Bluffton College, 1908—.

NOAH E. BYERS, A. M., Professor of Philosophy.

B. S., Northwestern University, 1898; Student, Chautauqua, N. Y., Summer School, 1898; Principal of Elkhart Institute, 1898-1903; Graduate student of Philosophy and Education, The University of Chicago, Summers of 1899 and 1900; Austin Scholar, Harvard University, 1902-03; A. M., Harvard University, 1903; President and Professor of Philosophy and Education, Goshen College, 1903-13; Dean and Professor of Philosophy, Bluffton College, 1913—.

C. HENRY SMITH, Ph. D., Professor of History and Social Sciences.

Student, Illinois State Normal, 1896-98; Instructor, Elkhart Institute, 1898-99; Student, University of Michigan, Summer 1899; A. B., University of Illinois, 1902; A. M., The University of Chicago, 1903; Phi Beta Kappa, 1903; Instructor, Goshen College, 1903-05; Fellow in History, The University of Chicago, 1905-07; Ph. D., The University of Chicago, 1907; Instructor, Illinois State Normal, Summer, 1907; Instructor, Manual Training High School, Indianapolis, 1907-08; Professor of History and Social Sciences, Goshen College, 1908-13; Dean of Goshen College, 1909-13; Professor of History and Social Sciences, Bluffton College, 1913—.

REV. JACOB H. LANGENWALTER, S. T. M., D. D., Professor of Practical Theology.

Student, Bethel College, Newton, Kansas, 1898-1900; A. B., German-Wallace College, 1904; Pastor of the First Mennonite Church, Halstead, Kans., 1905-09; B. D., Oberlin Theological Seminary, 1910; Acting President, Bethel College, 1910-11; Dean of the Bible Department, Bethel College, 1911-14; Graduate student, Harvard University, 1913-14; S. T. M., Hartford Theological Seminary, 1915; D. D., Baldwin-Wallace College, 1917; Professor of Practical Theology, Bluffton College and Mennonite Seminary, 1914—.

JOHN R. THIERSTEIN, Ph. D., Professor of German Language and Literature.

A. B., University of Kansas, 1896; Principal of Schools, Eudora, Kans., 1896-97; Superintendent of City Schools, Fredonia, Kansas, 1897-1901; Superintendent of City Schools, Osawatomie, Kansas, 1901-03; Professor of Mathematics and Mental Science, Bethel College, 1903-04; President Freeman College, Freeman, S. D., 1904-08; Graduate student, University of Bern, Switzerland, 1908-10; Ph. D., 1910; Principal of Atchison County High School, Effingham, Kansas, 1910-15; Professor of German Language and Literature, Bluffton College, 1914—.

REV. JASPER A. HUFFMAN, A. B., Professor of New Testament Language and Literature.

Graduate of B. D. course, Bonebrake Theological Seminary, 1909; Pastor, Dayton, Ohio, 1911-14; Editor, Gospel Banner, 1913—; Student, The University of Chicago, Summer, 1915; Instructor in New Testament Language and Literature, Bluffton College, 1914-15; Professor of New Testament Language and Literature, Bluffton College and Mennonite Seminary, 1915—.

JULIA ACKERMAN ADAMS, Mus. B., Professor of Theory and History of Music.

Mus. B., Wooster University, 1887; Student of W. S. B., Mathews, Chicago, 1895; Instructor in Music, Theil College, 1888-91; Lima College, 1893-1907; Professor of Theory and History of Music, Bluffton College, 1914—.

HARRY GEHMAN GOOD, Ph. D., Professor of Education.

A. B., Indiana State University, 1909; Harrison Scholar in Philosophy, University of Pennsylvania, 1909-10; University Scholar, U. of P., 1910-12; Ph. D., University of Pennsylvania, 1915; Head, Department of Mathematics, West Chester (Pa.) High School, 1911-12; Assistant Professor, Central High School, Philadelphia and West Philadelphia High School for Boys, 1912-15; Assistant Professor of Education, University of Oklahoma, Summer term, 1917; Professor of Education, Bluffton College, 1915—.

MARK EVANS, Mus. B., Professor of Singing.

Graduate, Ohio Northern University, Department of Music, under Hugh Owens, 1897; Studied under J. Cortland Cooper, Berlin, Germany; D. A. Clippinger, Chicago; W. W. Hinshaw, New York; Student, Cornell University, Summer, 1915; Conductor Bluffton Choral Society, 1909-13; Instructor in Singing, Bluffton College, 1910- 16; Professor of Singing, Bluffton College, 1916—.

REV. PAUL E. WHITMER, A. M., D. B., Professor of Church History.

A. B., Oberlin College, 1907; D. B., Oberlin Theological Seminary, 1908; Graduate Student in English, The University of Chicago, Summer of 1911, and the University of Michigan, 1912; Instructor, Goshen College, 1908-09;

Professor of Bible, Goshen College, 1909-12; Professor of English, Goshen College, 1912-16; Pastor of Goshen College Mennonite Church, 1910-13; Dean of Goshen College, 1913-16; A. M., The University of Chicago, 1917; Professor of Church History, Bluffton College and Mennonite Seminary, 1917—.

HARVEY EVERT HUBER, A. M., Professor of Biology.

A. B., Ohio Northern University, 1909; Teacher of Sciences, Glenwood, Colo., High School, 1909-11; A. M., Yale University, 1912; Laboratory Assistant, Yale University, 1911-13; Professor of Biology and Geology, Ohio Northern University, 1913-18; Professor of Biology, Bluffton College, 1918—.

GUSTAV ADOLF LEHMANN, A. B., Assistant Professor of Music.

Graduate Bluffton Academy, 1906; Teacher, Berne (Ind.) High School, 1909-10; Tri-State College, Summers, 1907-08; A. B., Earlham College, 1912; Instructor in German, Bluffton College, 1912-14; Dean of Conservatory of Music and Instructor in Singing and Theory, Bluffton College, 1914-16; Conductor Bluffton·College Choral Society, 1914—; Student with Sergei Klibansky, New York, Summers, 1914 and 1916; Assistant Professor of Music, 1916—.

HERBERT WELLER BERKY, A. B., Assistant Professor of Physical Sciences.

Graduate, Perkiomen Seminary, 1909; Instructor Perkiomen Seminary, 1908-09; A. B., Princeton University, 1913; Graduate student, University of Chicago, Summers, 1913, 1914, 1915 and 1916; Instructor in Physical Sciences, Bluffton College, 1913-16; Assistant Professor of Physical Sciences, 1916—.

SIDNEY HAUENSTEIN, Ph. C., Assistant Professor of String and Wind Instruments.

Student, Findlay College Conservatory of Music, 1898; Instructor in Violin, Defiance College, 1899; Director Bluffton Band, 1907-1915; P. S. C., University of Michigan, 1907; Conductor, Bluffton College Orchestra, 1911—; Instructor in String and Wind Instruments, Bluffton College, 1911-1918; Assistant Professor of String and Wind Instruments, Bluffton College, 1918—.

LEOLA PEARL BOGART, Assistant Professor of Pianoforte.

Student in Bluffton College School of Music, 1905-06; Findlay College, 1907-08; Cincinnati Conservatory of Music, 1908-09; Student with Frederick Maxson, Philadelphia, Summer 1916; Instructor in Pianoforte, Bluffton College, 1911-1918; Assistant Professor of Pianoforte, Bluffton College, 1918—.

GAIL WATSON, Assistant Professor of Violin.

Graduate of Chicago Musical College, under Hugo Heerman; Student in the Prague Bohemia Conservatory, under Stephen Sucby, one year; Student in Imperial Conservatory, Russia, under Leopold Auer, one year; Coached with Fritz Kreisler and Leopold Auer, 1918; Instructor in Violin, Bluffton College, 1914-1918; Assistant Professor of Violin, Bluffton College, 1918—.

EDITH McPEAK, A. B., Instructor in Latin and Greek.

Graduate, Bluffton Academy, 1904; Teacher, Bluffton Public Schools, 1904-10; Student, Bluffton College, 1910; A. B. Oberlin College, 1912; Instructor in Latin and Greek, Bluffton College, 1912—; Dean of Women, Bluffton College, 1913—.

* WILLIAM EGLY, A. B., Instructor in English.

A. B., Michigan University, 1913; Principal High School, Geneva, Ind., 1913-14; Principal, High School, Thatcher, Idaho, 1914-15; Graduate Student, University of Michigan, Summer School, 1915, 1916 and 1917; Instructor in English, Bluffton College, 1915—.

BOYD SMUCKER, M. O., Instructor in Oratory.

Graduate of School of Oratory, Goshen College, 1905; Student, Goshen College, 1905-06; Graduate of King's School of Oratory, 1906;Special Instructor at Waynesburg College, 1907-12; M. O., King's School of Oratory, 1908; Director of School of Oratory, Goshen College, 1907-13; Instructor in Oratory, Bluffton, 1915—.

ALICE MUELLER, A. B., Instructor in French and Spanish.

Student, Gymnasium, Bienne, Switzerland, 1909; Student, University of Bern, Switzerland, 1910-12; Teacher, High School, Ohio City, Ohio, 1913; Student, Wooster Summer School, 1913; Teacher, High School, Maumee, Ohio, 1913-14; A. B., Bluffton College, 1915; Graduate Student, The University of Chicago, 1917; Instructor in French, Bluffton College, 1915—.

* FRIEDA STREID, A. B., Instructor in Home Economics.

Student, Illinois Wesleyan College, 1911-12; Student, Bradley Institute, Summer, 1915; A. B., Bluffton College, 1916; Ph. B., The University of Chicago, 1917; Instructor, Home Economics, Bluffton College, 1916—.

OLIVER M. KRATZ, Physical Director and Instructor in History.

Graduate of Perkiomen Seminary, 1908; Student, Brown University, 1909-13; Instructor in History and Athletic Coach, St. Charles Academy, St. Charles, Mo., 1913-15; Instructor in English and Athletic Coach Peddie Institute, Heightstown, N. J., 1915-16; Physical Director and Instructor in History, Bluffton College, 1917—.

CECILIA N. KETTUNEN, Instructor in Art.

Graduate of Normal department, Art Institute of Chicago, 1917; Honorable Mention Certificate in charcoal and oil painting, Art Institute of Chicago, 1917; Student of Lorado Taft, Sr. Mantgelas, Wallcott, Charles Francis Brown, Louis Wilson; Teacher of painting, freehand and mechanical drawing, Hull House, Chicago, 1916-1917; Teacher of hand-work, Chicago Commons, 1916; Assistant Teacher in Art Institute, Public School teachers' class, 1917; Instructor in Art, Bluffton College, 1917—.

MARTIN W. BAUMGARTNER, A. B., Instructor in Clarinet.

A. B., Bluffton College, 1917; Supervisor of Music, Mt. Cory Public Schools, 1917; Supervisor of Music, Vaughnsville Public Schools, 1917—; Instructor in Clarinet, Bluffton College, 1916—.

ELIZABETH BOEHR, B. S., Instructor in Home Economics.
Student, Bethel College, Newton, Kansas, 1909-1911; Student, Peru (Nebr.) State Normal, 1912; B. S. University of Nebraska, 1917; Omicron Nu, 1917; Instructor of Home Economics, West Point (Nebr.) High School, 1917-18; Instructor in Home Economics, Bluffton College, 1918—.

SAMUEL T. MOYER, B. S., Instructor in Agriculture.
B. S., Penn State College, 1913; Graduate student, Bluffton College, 1917-18; Assistant in Agriculture and Biology, Bluffton College, 1917-18; Instructor in Agriculture, 1918—.

FLOYD PANNEBECKER, A. B., Instructor in Physics.
A. B., Bluffton College, 1917; Graduate student, Bluffton College 1917-18; Assistant Librarian, Bluffton College, 1917—; Instructor in Physics, 1918—.

* Absent on leave.

STANDING COMMITTEES OF THE FACULTY

Athletics
Mr. Kratz, Professors Smith, Berky

Commencement
Professors Lehmann, Whitmer, Huber, Miss McPeak

Catalog
Professors Byers, Hirschler, Langenwalter, Lehmann

Graduate Studies
Professors Thierstein, Hirschler, Smith, Good

Library
Mr. Egly, Professors Smith, Thierstein, Whitmer

Literary Societies
Professor Berky, Mr. Smucker, Miss Mueller, Miss McPeak

Publications and Advertising
Professors Smith, Good, Lehmann, Mr. Smucker

Recommendations
Professors Good, Thierstein, Huber

Registration and Advanced Standing
Professors Hirschler, Byers, Langenwalter

Religious Activities
Professors Langenwalter, Hirschler, Huffman, Miss Mueller

Scholarships
Professors Huffman, Thierstein, Byers, Hirschler

Student Affairs
Professors Byers, Lehmann, Miss McPeak

Social
Professor Whitmer, Miss McPeak, Miss Mueller

GENERAL INFORMATION

HISTORY AND ORGANIZATION

Bluffton College is an enlargement of Central Mennonite College, which was founded by the Middle District Conference of Mennonites.

For many years the need of such an institution was greatly felt by this Conference. As early as 1894 the matter was urged before the Conference. A school committee of three was appointed in 1896, and one of seven in 1897. The following year the present location was decided upon by the Conference and a board of nine trustees elected. In 1899 a constitution was adopted and the trustees authorized to erect necessary buildings and make all preparations for opening the school. On Tuesday, June 19,1900, the corner-stone was laid and on Wednesday, October 31, the same year, the building was dedicated. On Monday, November 5, 1900, the school was formally opened and work was begun on Tuesday, November 6, with an enrollment of twenty students. Only the Academic, the Normal, the Music and the Commercial departments were opened the first year. The first work in the College was done in the winter of 1903, and the first course in the Bible school was opened in the fall term of 1904.

On January 27, 1914, Central Mennonite College was transformed into the larger Bluffton College and Mennonite Seminary. The movement leading up to the present college organization had its inspiration in the conviction among several of the leaders in the education work of several branches of the Mennonite church that the young people of the church demand a well equipped, fully endowed, standard college, and a standard seminary where they might receive preparation for their life calling. Such an institution, it was felt, could be established only by co-operative effort.

As early as December, 1912, an informal meeting was held at the Hotel La Salle, Chicago, to consider the question. Those present at this meeting were President J. W. Kliewer of Bethel College, President N. E. Byers of Goshen College, President S. K. Mosiman of Central Mennonite College, and Rev. A. S. Shelly of Bally, Pennsylvania, of the Eastern Conference of the General Conference of Mennonites of North America. At this meeting it was tacitly agreed that any advanced work in education in the Mennonite church, if it is to serve the largest possible number of people, could best be accomplished by the co-operation of a number of branches of the church. It was further agreed that if sufficient interest in such a movement should manifest itself in several localities, a meeting should be called at some central place to consider the possibility of such an undertaking.

After some investigations had been made it was found that a number from several bodies of Mennonites expressed their willingness to attend a meeting to consider a union school movement in which the various branches of the church could unite. Accordingly a meeting was called to be held at Warsaw, Indiana, on May 29, 1913. Friends from the Mennonite Brethren in Christ, The Defenseless Mennonites, The Central Illinois Conference of Mennonites, The Old Mennonites and The General Conference Mennonites agreed to attend the meeting. Twenty-four friends of the movement attended the meeting. The most important resolution passed at this meeting was the following:

"Resolved, that it is the sense of this meeting that an institution be established, representing the various branches of the Mennonite church, giving the under-graduate and the graduate work of a standard college (courses leading to the A. B. and A. M. degrees), the theological and Biblical work of a standard seminary and courses in music aiming at the thorough development of the musical ability of our people and meeting the needs of our churches."

It was further resolved that the proposed institution should be established in connection with one of the schools already controlled by the Mennonite people and that the names of persons should be suggested who should be requested by those present to organize themselves into a Board of Directors to establish the proposed institution. Accordingly a Board of fifteen members was named by choosing three men from each of the above named bodies and this Board was requested to take the necessary steps in establishing this institution.

The first meeting of the Board was called for June the 24th, to be held at the Mennonite Home Chapel, Chicago. The roll call showed that from all of the five branches there were three members of the Board present, except one from which there were but two. Several members of the Board who could not be present sent substitutes.

At this meeting the Board formally organized itself by electing J. F. Lehman, Berne, Ind., President of the Board, Rev. E. Troyer, Normal, Ill., Vice-President, and C. H. Smith, Goshen, Ind., Secretary.

After a brief discussion it was unanimously decided that the proposed school should be established in connection with Bluffton College, Bluffton, Ohio. The name adopted for the new institution was "Bluffton College and Mennonite Seminary." A committee was appointed to take out a charter for the proposed school. A committee was also appointed to draft a constitution and by-laws. It was decided that there should be a Board of fifteen Trustees elected by the churches, three members from each body co-operating. The Alumni shall also elect three members on the Board and the Board shall have the privilege of electing three local men as associate members of the Board, and the President and Treasurer of the institution shall be ex-officio members of the Board. The Committee on Constitution was ordered to carry out these and other instruction and report at a later meeting of the Board.

It was decided at this meeting that upon favorable action by the Board of Trustees of Central Mennonite College the new Board would assume all the responsibilities and privileges of the former. Favorable action was taken later by the Middle District Conference and by the executive committees of both Boards. The report of the action of the two executive committees was made to and accepted by the joint meeting of the Boards of both Central Mennonite and the new Bluffton College on January 27, 1914, at which time Bluffton College and Mennonite Semniary began its legal and corporate existence as an institution of higher learning.

ARTICLES OF INCORPORATION
OF
BLUFFTON COLLEGE

First. The name of said corporation shall be **Bluffton** College.

Second. Said corporation is to be located at Bluffton in Allen County, Ohio, and its principal business there transacted.

Third. Said corporation is formed for the purpose of establishing, maintaining and conducting an institution of learning for the purpose of promoting education in all departments of learning and knowledge and especially in those branches usually comprehended in academic, collegiate and university courses: to acquire and hold for said purposes money, real estate, and other property necessary or proper to carry out said objects; and to do any and all things reasonable and necessary to be done to carry out said purposes. Such institution of learning is to be patronized and controlled by the various branches and conferences of the Mennonite Church in North America, but it shall be open to all on equal terms irrespective of creed.

Location

The College is located at Bluffton, Allen County, Ohio, a village with a population of about 2,000. The natural beauty of the place, together with such modern improvements as electric lights, complete telephone and water system, make Bluffton a desirable residence village. The Lake Erie & Western and the Northern Ohio railroads, two east and west lines, and the Western Ohio Electric Street railway from Cincinnati to Toledo through Bluffton greatly facilitate traveling conveniences for reaching Bluffton from any part of the country.

Bluffton has an elevation well above sea-level, a healthful climate, sanitary conditions, an abundant supply of good water, and the town is unsurpassed in healthfulness and freedom from epidemics. The numerous forest trees adorning the town make it a good retreat during the warm weather. It has a moral people, free from aristocratic display, and especially kind and courteous to students. There are no saloons in Bluffton, but there are plenty of good churches.

The College Campus is located on the west side of the village. It is a piece of rolling land of thirty-three acres, covered in places with a natural forest of oak, elm, beech, buckeye, maple, etc. The east side of the campus is traversed by the beautiful meandering, little stream known as Riley Creek. This little stream abounds in a wealth of material for Botanical and Zoological study, and is a very valuable asset to the College Campus. The soil of the Campus ranges from a light clay to a black loam.

Buildings

College Hall. The main building is a pleasant, conveniently arranged structure furnished with modern conveniences, heated with steam and lighted by electricity. The Hall is a three-story structure. On the first floor are located the toilet rooms and recitation rooms. On the second floor are recitation rooms and the college chapel. On the third floor are the college offices, recitation rooms and the Library.

The College Chapel is a nicely arranged room, with a good sized stage, and with a balcony, the whole with a seating capacity of about 500. It is equipped with a pipe-organ.

Science Hall. The Science Hall is a four-story structure, built of rough-faced pressed brick in the colonial style of architecture. The lower floor is devoted to the Department of Agriculture. It contains a soil testing laboratory, a room devoted to animal husbandry, a dairy room and a milk-testing laboratory, and a manual training shop.

The second floor contains a large hall which is used for a museum, a mathematics room, Botanical and Zoological laboratories, each connected with adequate store rooms, a lecture room, a reading room and a faculty room. In connection with this floor in an east annex to the building is located a conservatory, which adds materially to the usefulness of the Botanical laboratory.

Upon the third floor are two Chemical laboratories, both in connection with a lecture room and with draft closets for the removal of poisonous gasses, also with suitable store rooms. Two rooms are devoted to the Physics laboratory. This floor is also the home of the Home Economics Department, which occupies a series of apartments consisting of a cooking laboratory, a model dining room and a sewing room with an adjoining fitting room.

On the fourth floor are located halls for the four literary societies.

Ropp Hall. Ropp Hall is a four-story structure, built of rough pressed brick in the colonial style of architecture. In the front is a large porch or balcony that adds much to the comfort and attractiveness of the building.

On the first floor is a large, well-lighted spacious dining hall, with a capacity accommodating one hundred and fifty persons. There are also well equipped kitchen, pantry, store rooms and laundry on this floor.

On the second floor are located a spacious lobby and corridor, a large music room, a reception room, the Y. W. C. A. cabinet room, a guest room and suites of rooms for the Matron and Dean of Women, and instructors.

On the third and fourth floors are rooms for fifty girls, and in the attic are storage rooms for trunks, etc.

All floors of this hall have both tub and shower baths, all are heated by steam and lighted by electricity.

Music Hall. The Music Hall has a good location on the Campus; is a two-story frame building, the lower floor being entirely devoted to music, there being good rooms with pianos for studios and practice. The upper floor is occupied by men students, there being room to accommodate twelve. It is heated by steam and lighted by electricity.

Men's Cottage. The Men's Cottage is located near the Music Hall. It is a two-story frame structure, both floors being devoted to rooms for men. It is heated by steam and has electric lights and bath.

Gymnasium. The Gymnasium is a spacious building located on the campus. It is well lighted and well ventilated and contains hot and cold showers and electric lights. It also contains a splendid regulation size basket-ball court.

Laboratories

The Physical Laboratory is located on the third floor of Science Hall. It is a spacious room, well lighted and well ventilated. It is equipped with steam heat and electricity. The apparatus is of the most modern construction and in splendid condition. A dark room adjoins the laboratory.

The General Chemistry laboratory is situated on the third floor of Science Hall. It is fire-proof and modern in its construction, is well lighted and ventilated. It is equipped with 48 lockers. Each student has separate desk and is provided with water and sink. Another laboratory is equipped for work in Organic Chemistry, Qualitative and Quantitative Analysis.

The Zoology and Botany laboratories are located on the second floor of Science Hall. They are spacious rooms, well lighted and well ventilated. They are equipped with desks and lockers. Each student has a separate locker and is provided with a compound microscope, a small dissecting microscope and a case of dissecting tools. They are also equipped with sectioning apparatus, and contain a large collection of preserved specimens both Zoological and Botanical.

The Department of Home Economics is housed on the third floor of the Science Hall. It consists of kitchen, store room, dining room, sewing room with an adjoining fitting room.

The kitchen is a spacious, well lighted room, containing tables and lockers for twenty girls. Each table is supplied with two gas plates, cupboard and drawers for utensils, bread and meat boards and high stool. There is one enameled iron sink in each end of the kitchen.

Adjoining the kitchen is a small dining room in which practice meals are served.

The sewing room is supplied with sewing machines, tables for drafting and cutting, dress forms and various appliances for study of clothing.

Library

The Library contains a good supply of books for general reading and books used in class room work. There are several sets of the latest Encyclopedias, Dictionaries and Atlases. The reading room is supplied with the leading magazines and journals. Several funds supply sources each year for new additions to the Library.

Religious Life

It was the religious life rather than the educational interests of the friends of this College that gave rise to its establishment. It is the express desire of its earnest promoters to make it pre-eminently a Christian institution. The College believes with many others that religion is absolutely essential to complete manhood and womanhood. It believes in a loyalty to Christian truth that should manifest itself in a persistent and earnest application of that truth to the life of the world. It recognizes that all truth is one and that it is to be fearlessly welcomed, and that character is supreme.

Devotional services are conducted in the College chapel daily. All students of every department are required to attend these services.

There are seven churches in Bluffton, namely: A Methodist, a Presbyterian, a Disciple, a Lutheran, a Mennonite, a German Reformed, and a Roman Catholic. All students are required to attend divine services at least once on Sunday at any church which they or their parents may select.

Vesper services are held in the College chapel every second Sunday during the school year, at 3:00 o'clock. These services are conducted by members of the faculty and others.

Musical Advantages

Each year more colleges and universities are recognizing music in one or more of its branches as a legitimate and desirable part of a liberal education. Bluffton College has from the beginning emphasized the cultural value of music, and in its courses in music it has aimed to offer instruction that leads to an appreciation of this great art as well as to a comprehensive knowledge of it. College students may select some of the courses as electives for college credit. Besides this theoretic work, there are musical organizations open to students of all departments of the college.

The Choral Society meets each Wednesday night and sings in two concerts. The Messiah by Handel is sung at Christmas time and other programs and oratorios are given during Commencement week.

The Vesper Choir is open to students having attained a fair knowledge of music. A College Orchestra, composed largely of students, is heard in concert several times each year. Students with a certain degree of proficiency are admitted to this organization.

The Bluffton Citizens' Band offers opportunities to students who play quite readily. Opportunity for choir singing is found in practically every church in Bluffton.

The Music Course, consisting of three Artist numbers and two concerts by the College Choral Society, brings to the students the best in music. A list of these entertainments can be found in this catalog.

Numerous public and private recitals and entertainments offer excellent advantages to the students. All these advantages assist in the development of high standards in music and afford opportunities seldom found in much larger towns.

Student Organizations

The Student Senate is composed of representative students elected by the various student organizations and the general student body, with the faculty committee on student affairs as advisory members. Its purpose is to co-ordinate the interests of the various organizations, to assist the faculty in maintaining the highest standard of conduct among the students, and to give the students a voice in the general administration of the college. The faculty takes it for granted that the students are interested in maintaining the best conditions for life and work and believes that they can be of great assistance by co-operating in this manner.

Literary Societies have always been given a prominent place in the institution. At present the students of the college maintain four flourishing societies, as follows: Two societies for the ladies, the Philomatheans and Aletheans, and two for the men, the Adelphians and Athenians. These societies have established permanent headquarters on the fourth floor of the Science Hall, where each society has furnished a room for the use of its members.

The private and conjoint programs of these organizations have been a credit to their members. A friendly rivalry is already existing and the Literary Societies promise to be a prominent factor in the institution.

An annual oratorical contest is held under the auspices of the Intercollegiate Peace Society.

The College men have formed a triangular debating league

with Findlay and Ashland colleges, and the College women a dual league with Ohio Northern.

In these different organizations every student has ample opportunity for development along Literary lines.

Christian Associations. A Young Men's Christian Association, a Young Women's Christian Association and a Volunteer Band are maintained by the students of the College. These associations represent the moral and religious side of the College life of the student, and are of practical help to every man and woman of the institution. Meetings of the two Associations are held each week. The work of the various committees, the classes in Bible and Mission study, the touch with the world-wide problems and movements through all these make the Christian Associations most valuable auxiliaries to the spiritual life of the College.

The Witmarsum is the students' paper, published by an organization of students, the Press Club. The paper aims to serve as a means of bringing to present and former students the news of all student activities. The paper will also give the students who have it in charge good training in practical journalism.

The College Choral Society. This is the earliest musical organization in the history of the College and has been an exponent of good music at all times. The society each year furnishes two numbers on the College Music Course. Standard oratorios by the best classic and modern composers are sung with orchestra and artist solo talent. The society is open to students of all departments and to singers of Bluffton and community. Conservatory students pursuing a specified course are required to be in regular attendance at the weekly rehearsals of the society.

The College Orchestra. Open to students in all departments who have gained some proficiency in playing. Former students and musical friends in Bluffton and community are also invited to membership. Several concerts are given and the more advanced players appear in concerts with the Choral Society.

The College Glee Club. Open to men of the College, carrying successfully fifteen hours of work in any department. Membership is gained thru application to and examination by the Club Executive Committee, and upon vote of the club. Each member must be an active member of the College Choral Society or College Orchestra. The club purposes to develope the musical talent of members, to help spread the spirit of Bluffton College and to foster the feeling of good fellowship in the entire student body.

Athletics

Ample facilities are afforded for athletic purposes, and all proper encouragement is given for the maintenance of manly athletic sports. The school is provided with a gymnasium, a splendid athletic field and numerous tennis courts. Athletic matters are in the hands of the Athletic Association to which all students belong. A faculty committee, appointed each year, has supervision over all athletics and the Physical Director acts as coach for all college teams.

Extension Lectures

A majority of the members of the Faculty offer extension lectures upon subjects connected with their departments. The subjects are not of a technical character, but are of common interest. They have been prepared for high schools, teachers' meetings and institutes, commencement addresses, baccalaureate sermons, lecture courses, farmers' institutes, Sunday school conventions, etc. No charge is made beyond the actual expenses. Any one interested, address C. H. Smith, Secretary, Bluffton, O.

Admission

Bluffton College is open to all worthy students, irrespective of sex, race or church affiliations. Candidates for admission must be able to furnish satisfactory evidence of good moral character. Students coming from other schools must bring along certificates of honorable dismissal. The further requirements for admission are given in connection with the several departments. Students who do not wish to complete any course may select such studies as they are prepared to pursue.

Regulations

Students are entrusted with the private regulation of their general conduct under a high sense of personal responsibility, and in conforming to the special obligations resting upon them as members of the school. The Student Senate co-operates with the College officers in maintaining the conditions for the ideal life and good work.

LECTURES AND CONCERTS

March 18—Vesper Address—Rev. Frank Hartman, Celina.

March 29—Dual Co-ed Debate—O. N. U. and Bluffton.

April 1—Vesper Address—Rev. L. C. Mercer, Lima.

April 3—Dedicatory Recital, Harriet Humiston Organ, James H. Rogers, Cleveland, Organist.

April 13—Triangular Debate—Ashland, Findlay, Bluffton.

April 15—Vesper Address—Rev. F. H. Armacost, Fostoria.

April 20—Ohio Intercollegiate Peace Contest, Western Reserve Winner.

April 29—Vesper Address—Dr. Charles H. Clark, Supt. Lima State Hospital.

May 8—Bluffton College Orchestra Concert, Sidney Hauenstein Conductor.

May 13—Vesper Address—"The Religion of Browning"—Dr. S. F. Gingerich, University of Michigan.

May 18—Conservatory Graduating Recital—Miss Huldah Moser, Contralto; Harry L. Kohler, Bass; Miss Ella Welty, '18, Accompanist.

May 20—Organ Recital, Harriet Humiston Organ, Professor O. E. Hirschler, Organist, Albion College, Albion, Mich.

May 26—Conservatory Graduating Recital—Martin W. Baumgartner, Bass; Miss Leona Feltz, '16, Accompanist.

May 27—Annual Baccalaureate Address—"The Preparedness of the College Graduate"—President S. K. Mosiman, Ph. D.

May 28—Organ Recital, Harriet Humiston Organ, Professor H. B. Adams, Organist.

May 29—Annual May Day—Miss Mary Schumacher, '17, May Queen; Mid Summer Night's Dream by Mr. Smucker's Dramatics Class.

May 30—Commencement Concert—Mendelssohn's "Saint Paul" —Bluffton College Choral Society; Bluffton College Orchestra; Miss Estelle Lugibill, '20, Soprano; Miss Huldah Moser, '17, Contralto; C. O. Lehmann, '16, Tenor; H. L. Kohler, '17, Bass; Miss Pearl Bogart, Accompanist; G. A. Lehmann, Conductor.

May 31—Class Day Exercises; Alumni Banquet; Annual Meeting of the Board of Trustees.

June 1—Seventeenth Annual Commencement—Doctor J. G. K. McClure, President of McCormick Theological Seminary, Speaker; Commencement Luncheon, Professor E. J. Hirschler, Toastmaster.

June 13—Lecture—"Social Aspects of the Present Crisis"—Doctor Harry F. Ward, Boston Theological Seminary.

Sept. 12—Opening Address—"College Ideals"—Dean N. E. Byers.

Sept. 14—Faculty Recital—Mrs. H. B. Adams; Miss Gail Watson; Miss Pearl Bogart; Prof. H. B. Adams; Prof. G. A. Lehmann.

Sept. 16—Vesper Address—"Twentieth Century Christianity"—Rev. A. S. Watkins, D. D.

Sept. 24—Conservatory Recital.

Sept. 30—Vesper Address—Rev. C. W. Boucher, Lima.

Oct. 1—Artist Recital—Louis Kreidler, Baritone, Chicago Opera Association; Miss Pearl Bogart, Bluffton College, Accompanist.

Oct. 9—Artist Recital—Mrs. Rhea Watson Cable, Pianist; Miss Gail Watson, Violinist.

Oct. 14—Vesper Address—President W. H. Guyer, D. D. Findlay College.

Oct. 22—Conservatory Recital.

Oct. 28—Vesper Address—Rev. W. E. Verity, Bluffton.

Nov. 1—Matinee Recital—Music Faculty and Students—Lima Woman's Music Club.

Nov. 5—Conservatory Concert at Camp Sherman, Chillicothe, Ohio—Miss Gail Watson; Miss Pearl Bogart; Miss Estelle Lugibill; Miss Cleora Basinger; C. O. Lehmann; G. A. Lehmann.

Nov. 11—Vesper Address—Rev. G. J. Lapp, Dhamtari, India.

Nov. 15—Findlay Glee Club.

Nov. 20—Artist Recital—The Tollefsen Trio.

Dec. 3—Ellen H. Richards Day Program—Domestic Science Department, Miss Frieda Streid, Superintendent.

Dec. 11—Junior Play—"At the End of the Rainbow."

Dec. 12—Lecture—"True Americanism"—Doctor Edward A. Steiner.

Dec. 18—Annual Messiah Concert—Bluffton College Choral Society; Bluffton College Orchestra; Miss Estelle Lugibill, '20, Soprano; Miss Cleora Basinger, '21, Contralto; James Allen Grubb, Chicago, Tenor; Harry L. Kohler, '17, Bass; Miss Pearl Bogart, Pianist; G. A. Lehmann, Conductor.

Jan. 4—Organ Recital, Harriet Humiston Organ, Professor H. B. Adams.

Jan. 11—Missionary Lecture—Rev. George Verity, China.

Feb. 1—Annual Bible Lectures—Doctor E. M. Poteat, President of Furman College, Lecturer.

Feb. 12—Amateur Music-Recitation Contest.

Mar. 3—Vesper Address—"Archeology and the Bible"—Prof. J. A. Huffman.

Mar. 8 and 9—West Central Ohio High School Basket Ball Tournament.

Mar. 10—Conservatory Recital—Miss Leona Feltz, '16, Pianist.

Mar. 17—Vesper Address—Hon. N. W. Cunningham.

Mar. 22—Lecture—"The First American Expedition Across the Sahara"—Professor D. W. Berky of the Rockefeller Foundation and Sewanee University.

EXPENSES

Each new student is charged a matriculation fee of $1.00. This fee is payable only once.

No money will be refunded to the student who leaves before the close of the semester, except in cases where one is excused on account of his own illness, in which case one-half of the bills for the unexpired portion of the term will be refunded, provided the student has been in school for more than two and less than eight weeks.

A fee of fifty cents is charged for each extra examination in any course except such as are necessitated by sickness. This fee must be paid to the treasurer before the examination. Permission to take such an examination is granted by the Deans.

A fee of $1.00 is charged all matriculated students who

register on days later than registration day as designated by the calendar.

All tuition and special fees are listed with the description of work of the different schools.

BOARD AND ROOM

Board and room are payable in advance by the semester or half semester. First-class board is furnished at Ropp Hall at $3.25 per week. A rebate of $.25 per week will be given if paid in advance for half semester. These prices are subject to change if the food situation should grow worse. Rooms can be had at Ropp Hall and Men's Cottage from $1.00 to $1.25 per week. Students rooming alone pay 50 cents per week extra. These prices include heat, light, and the laundering of sheets, pillow-cases and towels. Students are required to mark their own linen.

Each room in the College halls is provided with all necessary furniture including single or double beds, mattresses and pillows. All other bedding, such as sheets, blankets, comforts and pillow-cases, also rugs, curtains, dresser and table covers, as well as table napkins are supplied by the student. A reservation charge of $5.00 is made to all students wishing to engage a room in any hall. This deposit must be made when the room is reserved, but it will be returned upon demand before August 1. Credit for this amount will be given upon the room rent of the first Semester.

All girls not living at home are expected to room at Ropp Hall unless excused by the Dean of Women.

All applications for rooms in Ropp Hall should be addressed to the Dean of Women. Rooms are filled in order of application; therefore, an early application is desirable.

SELF-SUPPORT

There are numerous opportunities such as, waiting table, janitor work, mowing lawns, firing furnaces, etc., for students who wish to earn at least part of their school expenses. In most cases, however, the student must apply in person to secure the work. The college can not promise to do this before the student enters college.

The Y. M. C. A. has an Employment Bureau which obtains

work for those who desire it and calls from the community for student labor are referred to them.

SCHOLARSHIPS

There is a scholarship from Gerhardt Vogt $1500.00 the interest of which is available for a student preparing for the ministry.

The Catherine C. Cromer Scholarship is an endowment of $1000.00, the interest of which is available for the payment of the tuition of a worthy and needy student in the College of Liberal Arts.

There are a number of scholarships available for students for the ministry or for students intending to do missionary work.

COLLEGE OF LIBERAL ARTS

FACULTY

Samuel K. Mosiman, President.

Noah E. Byers, Dean; Professor Philosophy.

Edmund J. Hirschler, Professor of Mathematics and Astronomy.

C. Henry Smith, Professor of History and Social Sciences.

John R. Thierstein, Professor of German Language and Literature.

Jacob H. Langenwalter, Professor of Practical Theology.

Jasper A. Huffman, Professor of New Testament Language and Literature.

Harry G. Good, Professor of Education.

Paul E. Whitmer, Professor of Church History.

Harvey E. Huber, Professor of Biology.

Gustav Adolf Lehmann, Assistant Professor of Music.

Herbert W. Berky, Assistant Professor of Physical Sciences.

Edith McPeak, Instructor in Latin.

* William Egly, Instructor in English.

Boyd D. Smucker, Instructor in Oratory.

Alice Mueller, Instructor in French and Spanish.

* Frieda Streid, Instructor in Home Economics.

Oliver M. Kratz, Physical Director and Instructor in History.

Cecelia Kettunen, Instructor in Art.

Elizabeth Boehr, Instructor in Home Economics.

Floyd Pannebecker, Instructor in Physics.

Samuel T. Moyer, Instructor in Agriculture.

* Absent on leave.

COLLEGE OF LIBERAL ARTS

The purpose of the College is to provide the instruction, activities, and stimulating atmosphere that will develop all the powers of the individual, introduce him to the great fields of knowledge, cultivate the true Christian character and prepare him to take his place as a useful member of society.

With this in view, the faculty is composed of members having high standards of Christian character and recognized teaching ability in addition to broad culture and thorough training in special fields obtained in the best universities in Europe and America.

The requirements for degrees prescribe some work in each of the large divisions of human knowledge and in addition some advanced work in one department, with enough electives to suit the peculiar needs of each student, thus giving liberal and specialized training adapted to the individual.

In order to aid the student to apply his general training to some useful vocation courses are offered in the various departments giving preliminary training for theology, medicine, law, engineering, journalism and business, and the departments of agriculture, domestic science and education give practical training in vocations in which our constituency is especially interested.

ADMISSION

Admission to the College of Liberal Arts may be obtained in one of two ways: First, by certificate; second, by examination.

By Certificate

Nearly all students enter the College by certificate from accredited high schools, academies or other prepartory schools. A candidate for admission must present evidence of his secondary school work in the form of an official detailed statement showing:

(a) The subjects studied by him and the ground covered.

(b) The amount of time devoted to each.

(c) The grades obtained in each subject.

Blank certificates of admission may be obtained on application to the Registrar of the College. These certificates should be filled out, signed and returned by the principal or superintendent of schools to the Registrar as soon as possible after the June commencement in order that it may receive the approval of the Committee on Admission before the student presents himself for admission.

Entrance Unit

Preparatory work is estimated in terms of the "entrance unit." A unit is the amount of work represented by pursuit of one preparatory subject with the equivalent of five forty-minute recitations a week for thirty-six weeks, or of four fifty-five minute recitations a week for thirty-six weeks. A laboratory period should be twice as long as a recitation period to count as the equivalent of one recitation.

Number of Units Required

Fifteen units are necessary for unconditional admission to the College. Students coming from high schools which compute their units in terms of a school year of thirty-two weeks must offer sixteen of these shortened units. A temporary deficiency of not more than two units will be permitted, but all such deficiencies must, if possible, be made up during the first year at college. Work done in making good deficiencies does not entitle to college credit, but does count in estimating the number of hours for which a student may register in one semester.

Required Units

The following units are required of all candidates for admission:

English .... 3 units
Foreign Languages .... 3 units
Mathematics .... 2 units
History .... 1 unit
Science .... 1 unit

If any student offers among the three units required in foreign languages a single unit in any one language, he shall be required to take another's year's work in that language before graduation.

Students may be admitted with less than three years of foreign languages, but for every year they are deficient, they shall be required to take six semester hours of foreign languages in the College in addition to the sixteen hours required of all students.

The remaining five units not prescribed shall consist of electives, and may be chosen from any subjects accepted for graduation by first-class preparatory schools.

DESCRIPTION OF ADMISSION UNITS

English

Three units of English work done in High School or its equivalent are required for admission. The student is expected to have read and studied enough of our best productions in English Literature to have given him an appreciation of further work to be pursued along those lines. If not enough credits can be shown for the work, an examination may be required and work in preparatory department if the student is deficient. The student must have some knowledge of Rhetoric in distinguishing the figures of speech and kinds of composition, etc., and also the use of the latter in grammatically correct and well punctuated and capitalized writing.

German

1. Counting Two Units.

A two-year preparatory course should include the completion of Becker-Rhoades' German Grammar, or its equivalent, a reader such as Gluck Auf, and 150 to 200 pages additional of simple prose from such books as Lohmeyer's Der Weg zum Gluck; Bluethgen's Das Peterle von Nurnberg; Grimm's Marchen; Leander's Traumereien; Stockle's Unter dem Christbaum; Gerstaecker's Germelshausen; Storm's Immensee.

The student should show the result of careful drill in pronunciation and ability to translate at sight easy German into idiomatic English, and simple English sentences into correct German.

History

One unit of History is required for admission. This unit may be selected from any of the following which should cover a full year of work, preferably as suggested by the Committee of Seven:

1. Ancient History.

    Such texts as West or Myers covering both the ancient nations together with Greece and Rome or such texts as Botsford's covering only Greece and Rome will be satisfactory, or any other work of an equal merit.

2. Medieval and Modern History.

    From the period of Charlemagne to the present. Work based on such texts as Myers, Robinson, West or others covering an equal field will be accepted.

3. American History and Government.

    Either a course in American History for a complete year or a course in History and Government will be accepted.

Latin

1. Counting Two Units.
    1. Latin lessons accompanied by the reading of simple selections.

    Caesar's Gallic War, books I-IV or its equivalent.
    3. Latin Prose Composition, the equivalent of one period a week, based on Caesar.

2. Counting Three Units.
    1. The above work, and in addition an amount of translation not less than Cicero; the orations against Cataline, for the Manilian law, and for Archias.
    2. Latin Prose Composition based on Cicero.

3. Counting Four Units.

    In addition to the preceding, Vergil's Aeneid, books I-IV or its equivalent.

Mathematics

The following statement gives a description of the contents of the three units usually taught in preparatory schools. It is advised that the order in which the subjects are taught be the same as the one given below. The second course in Algebra should follow Plane Geometry and be given not earlier than the third year.

1. Algebra, First Course.

    The four fundamental operations: factoring; H. C. F.

and L. C. M. by factoring; fractions, including complex fractions and the elements of ratio and proportion; linear equations, both numerical and literal, containing one or more unknowns, square root and radicals, numerical quadratic equations.

The pupil should be required throughout the course to solve numerous problems which involve the putting into equations of given data and conditions stated in words. Many of these problems should be chosen from mensuration, from physics and from practical life. The free use of graphic methods in connection with the solution of equations is also expected.—1 unit.

2. Plane Geometry.

The usual theorems and constructions of good text-books including the general properties of rectilinear figures; the circle and the measurement of angles; similar polygons; areas; regular polygons and the measurement of the circle.

Much practice should be given in the solution of original exercises, including problems in loci.—1 unit.

3 a. Algebra, Second Course.

Review of first year's course; radicals; exponents, including fractional and negative; extraction of the square root of numbers and of polynomials; general solution of quadratic equations with one unknown applied to literal as well as numerical co-efficients; simple cases of systems of equations that can be solved by the aid of quadratic equations; the solutions of quadratic systems by graphic methods; problems leading to quadratics, progressions; ratio, proportion and variation; logarithms.—½ unit.

3 b. Solid Geometry.

The usual theorems and construction of good text-books including the relations of lines and planes in space; the properties and measurement of prisms, pyramids, cylinders and cones; the sphere and spherical triangles.

Application to the mensuration of surfaces and solids.—½ unit.

Science

A year's laboratory work in any of the following sciences: Chemistry, Physics, Zoology, Physiology, or Botany. This must include both laboratory and text-book work, together equivalent to a full year's course in high school.

1. Chemistry.

The text-book requirement in Chemistry should cover the ground of such a text-book as McPherson and Henderson's Elementary Study of Chemistry. The student must present satisfactory evidence of having performed the experiments himself. The time devoted to laboratory work should be equal to that given to text-book work.

2. Physics.

In order to meet the requirements of Physics the student must have had text-book work equivalent to that given in Milliken and Gale, together with an adequate amount of actual laboratory work. The requisite amount of work in the laboratory is four hours per week throughout a high school year.

3. Zoology.

In satisfying the requirements in Zoology, the candidate may offer a year's work in such text-books as Needham's Elements, or Packard's Briefer Course. He must also present detailed information concerning the practical study of animals which he has made in connection with the study of the text-book.

4. Botany.

The requirements in Botany include the mastery of some such text-books as Bergen's Elements of Botany or Gray's Structural Botany and an adequate amount of laboratory and out-of-door study.

5. Physiology.

A full year's laboratory work with an approved manual.

PREPARATORY COURSES

Bluffton College does not maintain an academy, but for the present such courses as are required for College entrance will be offered for serious mature students who can adjust themselves to the conditions of college life and give evidence that they are qualified for the work. The courses are all given four hours each week during the year. Each course counts as one unit, and a certificate will be given upon the completion of fifteen units as prescribed for college entrance. The courses should be taken in the following order selecting four courses each year:

First Year	Second Year
Latin	Latin
Algebra	Geometry
English	English
Physical Geography	Ancient History

Third Year	Fourth Year
Latin	Latin
German	German
Physics	Algebra and Geometry
English	English
Domestic Science	Agriculture

REGISTRATION AND ENROLLMENT

All candidates for admission and all students intending to pursue their studies during the ensuing year should present themselves for registration on Tuesday, September 10, 1918. Students registering at a later date will be required to pay an additional registration fee of one dollar, unless a satisfactory excuse for the delay can be given. Registration for the work of the second semester will take place on Friday, January 24, 1919, with similar penalties for delay.

Method of Registration

The following order of procedure has been adopted to facilitate registration.

First—After having been duly admitted to College, the student obtains a registration card from the Registrar and in his presence fills out the blanks calling for general information concerning the student.

Second—A schedule of studies is then made out in the presence of the Dean or Faculty Advisor of the student. This having been done the Dean or Faculty Advisor places his signature upon the registration card.

Third—The student secures the signatures of the instructors of the various courses he has chosen.

Fourth—The student takes the card to the Business Manager of the College, and after making settlement for all tuition and fees receives his O. K. as evidence that all financial obligations have been met.

Fifth—The card is taken back to the Registrar from whom the student secures his class cards.

Sixth—The class cards are presented to the various instructors at the first recitation scheduled for each course. No student is enrolled as a member of a class until this has been done.

Admission to Advanced Standing

Students from other colleges or universities, who have pursued standard college courses equivalent to those of Bluffton College will receive credit for such courses upon presentation of proper certificates of creditable standing, and honorable dismissal, to the Faculty Committee on Advanced Standing. College credit will be given for work done in preparatory schools upon examination only.

Admission of Special Students

Persons of mature years who do not possess all the requirements for admission and are not candidates for a degree are permitted to enter the College of Liberal Arts upon giving satisfactory evidence to the instructors in charge that they are prepared to pursue to advantage the studies they desire.

Requirements for Graduation

A total of 120 semester hours of work is required for graduation in addition to the prescribed freshman lectures and 6 hours of physical training. One recitation per week for a semester of eighteen weeks constitutes a credit of one hour, provided a passing grade has been attained in the subject studied. The courses which a student may offer for graduation are divided into three classes: First, prescribed; second, major; third, elective.

Prescribed Courses

The prescribed courses are the following:
English Language and Literature.........10 hours.
Mathematics .... 6 hours.
Science (Physical or Biological) ....8 hours.

Ancient or Modern Languages..............16 hours.
Bible ....,.. 4 hours.
Philosophy and Education .... 6 hours.
History and Social Science ....8 hours.
Physical Training .... 6 hours.
Freshman Lectures .... 2 hours.

Latin or Greek may be substituted for Mathematics, hour for hour. Six hours additional work in Foreign Languages will be required for every unit in which the student is deficient in his entrance requirements for Foreign Languages.

All required courses with the exception of those in the Department of Philosophy and Education should be completed by the end of the Sophomore year. The requirements for the A. B. degree in Music are given in the description of courses in the Conservatory.

Major Courses

At the end of the Sophomore year each student is required to designate one department in which he intends to do the major part of his work. A major shall consist of not less than twenty-four hours of work completed in any one department. A major shall include the prescribed work in the department chosen.

Elective Courses

The remaining courses not included in either of the above groups are elective.

Students having completed 90 hours including all the prescribed and major courses may be granted a leave of absence during the Senior year in order to attend an approved professional school and will be given the A. B. degree after the completion of one full year of the professional course.

Amount of Work a Student May Take

The normal amount of work a student should take during one semester is 15 hours, not counting physical training or Freshman lectures. This will permit him to graduate after completing four years of work at the College. No student shall be allowed to register for more than 16 hours for one semester except by special permission of the Committee on Registration. Students who desire to take more than 16 hours must hand in a written request to this committee at least ten days before the close of the preceding semester specifying by name the courses they wish to take. Such requests can be granted only because of excellence in the work previously done at the college and then only on payment of an additional tuition fee of $2.00 for each hour of excess over 16. Under no conditions will a student be allowed to take more than 20 hours per week.

Grades

Students' grades are entered on the registrar's books on the following basis:

A—Excellent.
B—Good.
C—Average.
D—Passing.
E—Failed.
W—Dropped by consent of the Dean.
Inc.—Incomplete.

In accordance with the above schedule the lowest passing grade is D.

DEPARTMENTAL HONORS

1. A student may receive Departmental Honors in his major department only.
2. The student, at the beginning of his Junior year, is to make application in writing to his Major Professor. This application, with the Major Professor's recommendation, is to be submitted to the Faculty. Admission to candidacy is to be by vote of the Faculty.
3. The candidate is required to be in residence at Bluffton College during his Junior and Senior years, and to devote four full academic years to his College course.
4. In the candidate's major department he is to have no grades lower than B.
5. The Major Professor is to assign to the candidate extensive reading in the subject of his department or some large division thereof and to require the preparation of a thesis showing power in the organization of material but not necessarily the ability to do original work.
6. The candidate is to be required to pass a comprehensive examination upon his Major or upon that large division thereof in which his special work was done.

ANNUAL HONOR LISTS

At the close of each year the ROLL OF BLUFFTON SCHOLARS will be published. This includes the names of the students whose grades were A's and B's.

A second list called the BLUFFTON GRADE LIST includes all those students doing regular college work, who made no semester grades below D and who attained a grade of C or above in at least ⅔ of the hours taken.

ARRANGEMENT OF COURSES

Freshman—Required

English 1 and 2	2 hours
Mathematics or Ancient Languages	3 or 4 hrs.
Natural Science	4 hours
Language	3 or 4 hours
Physical Training	2 hours
Freshman Lectures	1 hour

Electives

History	3 hours
Bible	2 hours

Sophomore—Required

Language	3 hours
English 5 and 6	3 hours
History	3 hours

(If not taken in first year)

Bible	2 hours

(If not taken in first year)

Electives

Junior

All prescribed work, not taken in former years, completed,

THE ARTS-AGRICULTURE COMBINATION COURSE

Total time required, five years, three of which are to be spent at Bluffton College and two at the Ohio State University. At the end of four years' time the degree of Bachelor of Arts will be conferred by Bluffton College, and at the end of five years the degree of Bachelor of Science in Agriculture by the Ohio State University.

General **Requirements in Bluffton** College **of** Liberal Arts

1. No student is eligible for the Combined Arts-Agriculture Course who has not been a rsident student at the Bluffton College for at least three years and who has not gained at least 90 semester hours credit in Bluffton College.

2. No student shall be eligible for a degree from Bluffton College in the Combined Arts-Agriculture Course who has not received sufficient credit at the Ohio State University to complete a total of 120 semester hours of work.

3. The Faculty of Bluffton College reserve the right to refuse to recommend for the combined course any candidate who has, in their opinion not maintained a standard of good scholarship.

COMBINATION ARTS-AGRICULTURE COURSE

Three Years at Bluffton College

FIRST YEAR

First Semester		Second Semester	
English 1	2 hrs.	English 2	2 hrs.
Modern Language	4 hrs.	Modern Language	4 hrs.
Chemistry 1	4 hrs.	Chemistry 2	4 hrs.
Mathematics 3	3 hrs.	Mathematics 4	3 hrs.
Zoology 5	3 hrs.	Zoology 6	3 hrs.

SECOND YEAR

First Semester		Second Semester	
English 5	3 hrs.	English 6	3 hrs.
General Botany 3	4 hrs.	General Botany 4	4 hrs.
Modern Language 3 or	4 hrs.	Modern Language 3 or	4 hrs.
Chemistry 3	3 hrs.	Chemistry 4	3 hrs.
Bible	2 hrs.	Bible	2 hrs.

THIRD YEAR

First Semester		Second Semester	
Economics 17	3 hrs.	Sociology 18	3 hrs.
History 5	2 hrs.	History 6	2 hrs.
General Psychology 1	3 hrs.	Principles of Education	3 hrs.
Physics 9	4 hrs.	Physics 10	4 hrs.
Bacteriology	3 hrs.	Physiology	3 hrs.

Two Years at the Ohio State University
FOURTH YEAR

First Semester
Animal Husbandry 4
Agriculture Chemistry ... 4
Rural Economics 4
Agronomy 4

Second Semester
Choice of any two of these the fourth year. The remaining two the fifth year.

In addition to the two selected, at least ten hours to be elected with approval of the Advisor.

FIFTH YEAR

Two subjects of four required in Senior year.

Ten hours a week throughout the year, from any of the courses related to the previous year's work in the College of Agriculture.

DEGREES
Baccalaureate

The degree of Bachelor of Arts is conferred upon all studenst who have met the requirements for graduation from the College of Liberal Arts.

Higher Degrees

The College offers to graduates of Bluffton College or other standard colleges opportunities for a year of graduate study leading to the A. M. degree.

Requirements for the A .M. Degree

The requirements for the A. M. degree are the following: A year of resident graduate study together with the completion of a sufficient amount of work in advanced courses to entitle the student to 30 hours credit. All credits must be of either A or B grade. Fifteen hours of work must be completed in one department of instruction which shall constitute the student's major work. These fifteen hours shall include the writing of a satisfactory thesis upon some subject chosen from the candidate's major department. The thesis shall count for five hours credit. The remaining fifteen hours may be selected from not more than two related departments.

Application for the degree shall be made at the time of enrollment in September. In this application the candidate shall designate the department in which he intends to do his major work.

The undergraduate requirements shall include the completion of a major of twenty-four hours in the department in which graduate work is desired.

The thesis, when finished, is to give evidence of the candidate's power of research and of an adequate mastery of his major subject. The subject of the thesis is to be chosen in consultation with the major professor and filed with the registrar on or before December 1.

The thesis is to be finished by May 1 in three type-written copies, one of which is to be in bound form, to be filed in the College library, another goes to the major professor, and the third is for the candidate's own use.

All candidates for the Master's degree are required to possess a reading knowledge of either German or French.

All graduate courses must be submitted for approval to the Committee on Graduate Studies of the College of Liberal Arts, upon whose recommendation also the Faculty will principally rely in awarding the degree. With the consent of this committee the candidate for the Master's degree may select all or a part of his year's work from departments in the Mennonite Seminary.

The candidate is given a final oral examination covering all the courses offered for the degree conducted by the heads of the departments in which he does his work.

Graduates of Bluffton College may be permitted to do a limited amount of the work for the Master's degree in other standard institutions, provided the approval of the Dean of the College of Liberal Arts and the head of the department in which the major is to be done has been secured in advance.

A fee of five dollars will be charged for the diploma.

DEPARTMENTS OF INSTRUCTION

The work of the College is organized under fifteen Departments of Instruction, alphabetically arranged as follows:

    I. Agriculture .... Ag.
    II. Ancient Languages .... A. L.
    III. Art .... A.
    IV. Biblical Literature .... B.

V. Biological Sciences .... B. S.
VI. Education .... Ed.
VII. English .... E.
VIII. History and Social Sciences .... H.
IX. Home Economics .... H. E.
X. Mathematics and Astronomy .... M.
XI. Modern Languages .... M. L.
XII. Music .... Mu.
XIII. Philosophy .... P.
XIV. Physical Sciences .... P. S.
XV. Physical Training .... P. T.

First semester courses are given odd and second semester even numbers. The number of hours credit is indicated in each course. An hour is one class period a week for one semester or the equivalent in laboratory work.

I. AGRICULTURE

Mr. Moyer

The courses in Agriculture aim to prepare teachers in this subject for the public schools. Course One gives outline of subject matter and Course Two gives methods of teaching.

1. General Agriculture   Three Hours, First Semester
    This course will deal with the elementary principles of Agriculture. It is designed primarily to give students a general knowledge of the subject. The subjects discussed will be: The Improvement of Plants and Animals, Propagation of Plants, Plant Food, The Soil, Maintaining the Fertility of the Land, Some Important Farm Crops, Enemies of Farm Crops, Systems of Cropping, etc.

2. Teaching Agriculture in the High School.
                             Three Hours, Second Semester.
    This course will give a survey of the work being done in Secondary Agriculture in the schools. It will take up materials for class room work and laboratory work; show how to arrange them in pedagogical way, so that recitations, lectures, and supplementary work will bring the pupils into vital contact with the material objects and the natural phenomena.

Short Agricultural Course

A short course in Agriculture will be given again next winter. A special bulletin is to be issued announcing the work to be offered. A certificate is given for three years' work, in this course. Those desiring information for short course, address Bluffton College, Bluffton, Ohio.

II. ANCIENT LANGUAGES

Greek

The aim in the instruction in Greek is to give the students the mastery of the elements of Greek Grammar and a fair knowledge of the language, which will prepare them for more advanced reading. The students are drilled in accurate pronunciations, a clear Greek hand, and in the essentials of vocabulary, inflection and syntax. There is daily composition in all classes from the very beginning.

Professor Huffman

1-2. Elementary Greek. **Four Hours, Two Semesters.**

White's First Greek Book, one book of Anabasis and some New Testament. Texts: Kelsey's Anabasis, Collar and Daniel's Greek Composition, Goodwin's Greek Grammar.

Miss McPeak

3-4. Second Year Greek. **Four Hours, Two Semesters.**

The reading of the Anabasis, II-IV. Review of Grammar, Prose Composition. Gulick's The Life of the Ancient Greeks will be read and studied in this course. Daily composition. Sight reading. Translations from the Anabasis, Books V-VII or Homer's Iliad.

Latin

Courses 11 to 14 are designed for students entering with two units of Latin and should be elected in the Freshman year. It is with the aim of giving the student a general knowledge of the Latin language and literature that the courses in this department are offered. Students, planning to do major work in Latin, should take some work in Greek, at least Greek 1-2.

Miss McPeak

11-12. Cicero.   **Four Hours, Two Semesters.**
Selected Orations.

13-14. Vergil. Aeneid.   **Four Hours, Two Semesters.**

15. Cicero, de Senectute.   **Four Hours, First Semester.**

16. Horace Odes and Epodes.   Four Hours, Second Semester.
Livy Selections from Books XXI and XXII.

17. Pliny. Letters (Not given 1918-1919)
Three Hourse, First Semester

18. Tacitus, Agricola and Germania. (Not given 1918-1919.)
Three Hours, Second Semester.

19. The Private Life of the Romans.
Two Hours, First Semester.
Lectures upon the daily life of the ancient Romans,
classes of society, family, marriage, dress, education, trade,
amusements, death, burial; a study of the Roman private
house.   Outside reading will be required.

20. Latin Writing.   **Two Hours, Second Semester.**
Systematic review of Latin Grammar and Exercises that
involve constant application of those rules of Syntax.

21-22. Lucretius. Books V and VI. (Not given in 1918-1919)
Two Hours, Two Semesters.

24. Teachers' Training Course.   **Two Hours, Second Semester.**
This course is intended to assist students in preparing to
teach Latin effectively in secondary schools.   Methods of
teaching paradigms, translation, vocabulary, etc., will be
discussed; also the comparative merits of different text-
books; a list of the books necessary for the library of a
teacher of Latin will be given.

A text-book will be used for the study of pronunciation,
hidden quantity, orthography, syntax.—Bennett's "The Latin Language."   Open to Seniors majoring in Latin.

III. ART

Miss Kettunen

The art department is divided into three distinct classes of
instruction:

1. Normal art instruction.
2. General art.
3. Lecture courses on history of architecture, sculpture, painting and ornament.

1. The normal classes are for students who plan to teach in the grade schools or for music students who are going to teach music in schools and might be required to take charge of the art department also.

2. The general art course includes freehand drawing, mechanical drawing, work in crayon, water color and oils, china painting, design, crafts, costume design, house plans and composition. College credit to the extent of four hours is given provided the student has had work amounting to one year's work prescribed in this department. One hour of credit is given for two hours of practical work.

3. The lecture courses in art are given for the benefit of students desiring a theoretical knowledge of art. College credit is given for these courses.

Instruction in class 2 is adapted to the individual needs of each pupil who is advanced according to his own progress.

Work completed must not be taken from the studio without instructor's permission. An exhibition of the students' work is held during the last week of school in the spring.

Students are required to furnish their own material— there being no laboratory fees.

1. **Normal Art.**   **Two Hours, First Semester.**

Methods of teaching drawing in grades 1-6. Mediums— chalks, water color, charcoal. Method — imagination and past observation. Subjects — landscape, animals, birds, flowers, interiors, holidays, fruits and vegetables. Four hours practical work, one hour lecture.

2. **Normal Art.**   **Two Hours, Second Semester.**

Methods of teaching handwork in grades 1-6. Mediums —reed, raffia, weaving, paper construction and whittling. Method—imitation and dictation. Subjects—baskets, mats, etc. Paper Construction correlated with drawing. Four hours practical work, one hour lecture.

3. Free Hand Drawing.

Charcoal, pencil, pen and ink.

a—Drawing of cast fragments in charcoal, outlining of values, shading.

b—Work from experience in pencil. Present observation—landscapes, figures, flowers, still life, fruits and vegetables.

c—Same as b worked out in pen and ink.

4. Mechanical Drawing.

Intersections, penetrations, isometrics, oblique, and dimetric drawing, orthographic projections, lettering, developments, intersections and working drawings.

5. Water Color, Oils and Crayon.

Pre-requisite—three months course 3 if there has been no previous work in drawing. Color class-composition, light effects, color effects, perspective, study of color. Studies—present observation of still life, flowers, landscapes, etc.

6. China Painting.

Prerequisite, history of ornament lectures.

7. Crafts.

History of ornament lectures required. Leather painting, leather tooling, book-binding, stenciling, reed and raffia work, stick and block printing.

8. House Plans.

Home planning from artistic and economical point of view. Lecture and laboratory course. History of ornament.

9. Composition.

1—Masses of values, placing, balance, harmony, handling of subject.

2—Decorative and pictorial composition.

3—Application of decorative, screens, wall panels and lamp screens.

4—Pictorial, themes of weather, time, sound, objects, figures, landscapes and interiors.

11. History of Architecture and Sculpture.

Two Hours, First Semester.

Egyptian, Assyrian, Greek and Roman architecture and

sculpture. Early Christian, Byzantine, Mohammedan, Romanesque, Gothic and Renaissance architecture.   Italian Renaissance sculpture. Modern sculpture.

12. History of Painting.   Two Hours, Second Semester.
    Italian painting thru the Renaissance period with an introductory study of Egyptian, Greek and Roman painting. French,. Spanish, Flemish, Dutch, German, English and American painting. Chinese and Japanese art.

IV. BIBLICAL LITERATURE

The influence of the Bible upon History, Literature and Music, as well as upon the development of noble, human character has been so great and far-reaching that one naturally considers at least a fair acquaintance with this book essential to a liberal education.   The colleges are, more and more, expected to furnish the leaders for society.   In order to do this they must develop leaders, men with character, as well as knowledge.   Such an obligation has naturally led educators to recognize with new emphasis the value and importance of definite and thorough Bible study.

Professor Huffman

5. Pentateuch and Historical Books. Two Hrs., First Semester
   Special attention will be given to the Pentateuch, and as much time as possible will be devoted to the other Historical Books.   Recent archaeological discoveries will be studied in their relation to the historical and scientific accuracy of the Bible.

6. Prophecy, Psalms and Wisdom Literature.
                             Two Hours, Second Semester.
   Prophecy will be studied especially in relation to its messianic aspect.   The student will be familiarized with Hebrew poetry. The Wisdom Literature will be studied with special attention devoted to the Book of Job.

7. Harmony of the Gospels.   Two Hours, First Semester.
   The four gospels will be studied in their relation to each other, as well as individually. The events recorded will be brought together in one harmonious whole, each one of the Gospels making its contribution to the record of our Lord's earthly ministry.   Kerr's Harmony of the Gospel will be used. Not given 1918-19.

8. Acts and Epistles.   **Two Hours, Second Semester.**
The beginning of the Christian Church as recorded in the Acts will be carefully reviewed. The Missionary Labors of the Apostle Paul will be followed, and his epistles to the various churches established will furnish a doctrinal basis for study. The Bible will be the principal text-book.
Professor Whitmer

9-10. Old Testament Literature.   **Two Hours, Two Semesters.**
This is a reading course covering the whole of the Old Testament in English. It seeks to do five things: To give a knowledge of the types of literature represented in the Old Testament; to re-create the living historical background out of which the Old Testament grew; to give familiarity with the literary structure and composition of each book; to discover the point of view and purpose of each writer; to make the Bible a vital force in the life and thought of the present day. Designed primarily for College Sophomores. Not given 1918-19.

11-12. New Testament Literature. **Two Hours, Two Semesters.**
The purpose of this course is to give an intimate acquaintance with the New Testament writings. Each book is considered with respect to its historical setting, literary character, author, first readers, occasion, aim and social, ethical and religious teachings. Designed primarily for College Sophomores.
Professor Langenwalter

13-14. Modern Problems in the Light of the Old Testament.
Two Hours, Two Semesters
The question is often raised whether the Old Testament has any contribution to make to the solution of modern social and ethical problems. It is the purpose of this course to make a thorough study of those portions of the Old Testament which deal with such problems in order to find what suggestions they may contain bearing upon a possible solution of the problems of our own day. Designed primarily for College Juniors.

15-16. Modern Problems in the Light of the New Testament...
Two Hours, Two Semesters
Portions of the New Testament, dealing with social and

ethical problems, will be carefully investigated for the purpose of finding any suggestions they may have to offer for the solution of similar problems today as these confront the thinking man. Designed primarily for the College Juniors. Not given 1918-19.

3-4. Christian Ethics. **Two Hours, Two Semesters**
This course will involve a study of the development of ethical thought arising from the use of the Christian Scriptures; a comparison of the type of ethics evolved from the application of the principles of Christian ethics to the problems of modern society. Open only to Seniors and graduate students, except by special arrangement.

V. BIOLOGICAL SCIENCES
Professor Huber.

The influence that the Biological Sciences have had in the past, are having in the present, and are going to have in the future on the development of civilization, justify them a place in the curriculum of a College of Liberal Arts.

The aim of all work in Biology is to give the student a better idea of the relation of the living world to human life. In order to give one a better idea of life, it should have as central idea or factor, man; should consider all functions in their relation to human life, and should consider better ways of carrying on their own lives and of helping to improve the surroundings in which they live. A secondary aim is to prepare students to teach the Biological Sciences, and to give students a working knowledge for advanced work in these lines.

The laboratories are equipped with dissecting and compound microscopes and other appliances. In addition to the above equipment the greenhouse and acquarium are valuable adjuncts to the department, furnishing much fresh material for laboratory use and for carrying on special work when growing plants are used. Lecture room is furnished with a lantern for the projection of transparent slides and opaque objects.

1-2. General Biology. **Three Hours, Two Semesters.**
An introductory course presenting the fundamental principles of the living organism. This course should develop the scientific habit of mind and prepare the student for ad-

vanced work.   Both theoretical and practical problems of
the living world are discussed.   Some of the topics treated
are: the origin and nature of life, cellular organization,
food manufacture, metabolism, growth, reproduction, differentiation, decay, heredity, environment.   First semester,
Plant Biology; second semester, Animal Biology.   Recitation 2 hours, laboratory 4 hours.

3-4. Botany.   Four Hours, Two Semesters.
    A course in the structure and functions of plants. Spec-
ial emphasis is placed upon the economic aspects of botany.
Lectures and laboratory throughout the year; field work
during fall and spring.   First semester, Algae, Fungi, Liv-
erworts and Mosses; second semester, Ferns, Clubmosses,
Horsetails and Seed Plants with special attention to the latter.   Lecture and recitation 2 hours, laboratory 4 hours.
Prerequisite, Plant Biology.

5. Invertebrate Zoology.   Three Hours, First Semester.
    A course devoted to the study of the classification, struc-
ture, behavior, distribution, economic importance and life-
histories of the invertebrates.   Types of the important
groups are studied in the laboratory. Lecture and recitation 2 hours, laboratory 4 hours. Prerequisite, Animal Biology.

6. Comparative Anatomy.   Three Hours, Second Semester.
    A comparative study of the vertebrate plan of structure.
Dissections are made of typical vertebrates with special attention to the mammal.   Anatomy of organs is correlated
with origin and function.   This course, with Invertebrate
Zoology, is especially recommended for those intending to
teach Biology or those who expect to enter medical schools.
For the general student these courses develop a better appreciation of the relation of man to the animal world. Lecture and recitation 2 hours, laboratory 4 hours.

7. Bacteriology.   Three Hours, First Semester.
    A lecture and laboratory course presenting the funda-
mental principles of bacteriology. Media, sterilization, cul-
tures, staining, isolation and identification are studied. Emphasis is placed upon the relation of bacteria and other mi-

cro organisms to the farm, the home and the medical sciences. Classroom 2 hours, laboratory 4 hours.

8. **Plant Pathology.**   **Three Hours, Second Semester.**

A study of the diseases of plants. Investigations of injury or diseases caused by fungi, bacteria and insects. Recitations 2 hours, laboratory and field work 4 hours. Prerequisites, Botany and Bacteriology. Not given 1918-19.

9. **Embryology.**   **Three Hours, First Semester.**

A course designed to acquaint the student with the development of an animal from the germ cells to the formation of its organs. Attention is given to the origin of the germ cells, fertilization, cleavage, differentiation of tissues and organs, theories of growth, heredity and inheritance. Lecture and recitation 2 hours, laboratory 4 hours. Prerequisites, Courses 1-2, 5 and 6. Not given 1918-19.

10. **Human Physiology.**   **Three Hours, Second Semester.**

A course dealing with the structure and functions of the human body. Hygiene is given due consideration. Recitations, demonstrations and laboratory work. Prerequisite, Biology 1-2.

12. **Sanitation and Public Health. Two Hours, Second Semester.**

This course treats topics like these: germ theory of disease, infectious and non-infectious disease, prevention of disease, predisposing and specific causes of disease, environment factors conducive to the spread of disease, susceptibility and immunity, old and new public health practices, sanitary surveys. Not given 1918-19.

13. **Historical Technique and Biological Methods. Three Hours.**

A practical course for students who intend to teach biology or do graduate work. Methods of collecting, killing, preserving and preparing material for demonstration and laboratory purposes are considered. Students become familiar with the microtomes and their uses. Careful attention is given to the principles and methods of imbedding, staining and mounting. Problems which are likely to be met in the biological laboratory of secondary schools are discussed. Lecture and recitation 1 hour, laboratory 6 to 8 hours.

Prerequisites, Courses 1-2 and 3-4 or 5 and 6. Not given 1918-19.

Courses recommended for professional preparation:

Teaching:—Courses 1-2, 3-4, 5 and 6, 9, and 12.

Agriculture and Forestry:—Courses 1-2, 3-4, 7 and 8.

Nursing:—Courses 2, 5, 6, 7, 9, and 11.

Premedical:—Courses 1-2 or 5 and 6.

VI. EDUCATION

Professor Good

The department offers courses for teachers of both the elementary and the secondary grades. These courses meet the requirements for professional preparation in Ohio and elsewhere. Prospective candidates for teaching positions should acquaint themselves with the various state requirements concerning the work in Education, especially with reference to certification.

Those who wish to major in Education will select their courses for the major with the advice of the head of the department. Several of the courses in the Departments of Philosophy and Sociology may be counted towards a major in Education Attention is also called to the courses in Special Methods offered by the various departments.

Education 1 and Education 2 are courses introductory to the general field of Education and should be taken first.

1. **The History of Education.   Three Hours, First Semester.**

    This course is intended to be an introduction to the study of the general educational problem. The emphasis will be placed upon the ideals of past times and upon movements and institutions rather than upon the work of individuals. However, the influence of such representative thinkers as Plato, Quintilian, Comenius, Locke, Rousseau, Pestalozzi, Herbart and Spencer will illustrate these larger topics. Text, readings and reports.

2. **Modern Educational Theory. Three Hours, Second Semester.**

    This is a course in the principles of education and is continuous with the History of Education. It treats the aim, content, values and ideals of education as set forth by the leading educational thinkers of the present day. The course should, by discussion and wide reading, give the student command of a fundamental set of consistent principles to guide in further study and work.

3. Method.   **Three Hours, First Semester.**

Both general and special method will be treated. Attention will be given to the methods of drill, of habit-formation, of memory work, of reasoning and of appreciation, of lesson-planning and the testing of results.

4. School Management.   **Two Hours, Second Semester.**

The organization and management of the school, the problems of interest and attention, the daily program, class-management and discipline will be treated. More attention will be paid to practical than to theoretical topics.

5. Secondary Education.   **Three Hours, First Semester.**

The organization, administration and methods of teaching applicable to the American high school will form the subject matter of this course. Several texts will be used, such as the works of Brown, Stout, Hollister and Parker.

6. Educational Classics.   **Two Hours, Second Semester.**

This is a reading course intended to give students a first-hand acquaintance with some of the important educational classics. This year, Plato and Aristotle, some of the English writers, Ascham, Mulcaster, Milton and Locke, together with Comenius, will be read. Prerequisite Education 1.

7. The Rural School.   **Two Hours, First Semester.**

The aim in this course will be to outline a constructive program for the improvement of the rural school. This will involve a discussion of the rural educational needs and of the possible readjustments of equipment and curricula to meet these needs. References will be made to the best of the rapidly growing literature on rural education.

8. School Administration.   **Two Hours, Second Semester.**

This is a descriptive course in general school administration. Dutton and Snedden's The Administration of Public Education in the United States is used as a text.

10. Elementary Observation.   **Two Hours, Second Semester.**

The observation in the grades is supplemented by conferences and reports.

11. Elementary Practice. **Two Hours, First Semester.**

This work is under the direction of a critic teacher with the supervision of the Department of Education. Lesson plans are required and constructive criticism is given.

12. Secondary Observation and Practice.

Three Hours, Second Semester.

The students observe under direction the teaching of their major and minor subjects in the high school. Each student is then required to do six weeks of actual class room teaching under supervision.

14. Educational Measurements. **Two Hours, Second Semester.**

This course will treat the deriviation of scales and their use in education; the study of some of the important education surveys; and the application of this knowledge to some practical problems of educational method or administration.

15-16. Special Methods. **Both Semesters.**

Each semester one course of two or three hours is offered in the methods of teaching an elementary school subject. These courses are required in the two-year elementary school course but no college credit is earned by completing them. The following courses are offered: Arithmetic and Methods; Geography and Methods; Grammar and Methods; Reading and Methods.

A course in Primary Reading is also given in the second semester by Miss Verena Hilty of the Bluffton Public Schools.

VII. ENGLISH
* Mr. Egly

Mr. Smucker

The work in the Composition and Rhetoric courses is intended to give the student practice in writing the different types of prose composition. The aim is to secure correctness and clearness of expression.

The general courses of English and American Literature aim to open the field of Literature to the student. The purpose

* Absent on leave.

of the courses is to give the student a general historical outline and to show the different stages of development. The characteristics of the different periods are pointed out which serves as preparatory work to a more minute study of special periods. The work is intended to awaken the student's appreciation for literature.

1-2. Composition. **Two Hours, Two Semesters.**
The work in this course is intended to develop the student's power of expression. Considerable attention is given to the details of composition. Themes are written weekly throughout the year. Required Freshman course.

3-4. Rhetoric. **Two Hours, Two Semesters.**
This is an advanced course in the study of Rhetoric. Genung's "Working Principles" will be used as a text. Open to all students who have had Courses 1 and 2.

5-6. History of English Literature.
Three Hours, Two Semesters.
This course is a survey of the English writers from the beginning of English Literature to the present. A historical outline is followed in the course of study, with assigned readings from the different writers. Not open to Freshmen.

7-8. History of American Literature.
Three Hours, Two Semesters.
A brief review of the leading American writers and a study of some of the leading works of each. Outside readings will be assigned with class reports.

9-10. Nineteenth Century Poetry. Three Hours, Two Semesters.
An intensive study will be made of the poetry of this important period of English Literature, especially emphasizing the works of Wordsworth, Tennyson and Browning.

11-12. Shakespeare. **Three Hours, Two Semesters.**
This course will be a detailed study of at least six of Shakespeare's plays. The relation of his work to the literature that preceded and followed will be taken up. Not given 1918-19.

13-14. Novel Course. **Two Hours, Two Semesters.**
History of the early forms of prose narratives and the beginnings of the English novel and a thorough study of the

18th century masters of the novel. Assigned readings and reports required.

19-20. American Dramas.   Three Hours, Two Semesters.

This course will deal with American plays, written and acted by Americans. The aim of the course is to show the development of the American drama from its beginning to the present day. Not given 1918-19.

Professor Whitmer

11-12. The Bible in Literature.   Three Hours, Two Semesters.

The chief object of this course will be to trace and evaluate the Biblical and ethical ideas in several great literary masterpieces. The following selections are representative of the masterpieces to be studied: Dante's "Divine Comedy," Shakespeare's "Sonnets," "King Lear" and "Macbeth," Miltons "Paradise Lost," Wordsworth's "Intimations of Immortality," Goethe's "Faust," Tennyson's "In Memoriam" and Browning's "Saul," "Rabbi Ben Ezra" and "A Death in the Desert." Not given 1918-19.

Open to Seniors and qualified Juniors.

13-14. Bible in Modern Prose.   Three Hours, Two Semesters.

A closer acquaintance with the prose literature which deals with life problems and ideals is the chief aim of this year's work. The works studied will be selected from the following: Johnson's "Rasselas," Eliot's "Romola," De-Quincey's "Confessions," Reade's "Cloister and the Hearth," Carlyle's "Sartor Resartus," Newman's "Apologia pro Vita Sua," Thackeray's "Vanity Fair," Arnold's "Culture and Anarchy," Hugo's "Les Miserables," and Tolstoy's "Anna Karanina."

Open to Seniors and qualified Juniors.

Public Speaking

15. Practical Elocution Course.   Two Hours, First Semester.

The fundamentals of Public Speaking are emphasized in this course. Special attention is given to pronunciation, tone placing, posture and gesture. Selections will be committed and recited before the class. "Fulton and Trueblood" will probably be used as text.

16. Argumentation and Debate.   Two Hours, Second Semester.
Gardner's "The Making of Arguments" will probably be used as a text with practical work in the class room for delivery.

VIII. HISTORY AND SOCIAL SCIENCES
Professor Smith
Mr. Kratz

The purpose of the Department of History is to give the student a correct conception of the forces and movements in the past life of human society which have contributed most largely to our present political, social, economic and religious institutions.   In the study of the past the present is always kept in mind, and those phases of past history which have done most to shape our modern life are given attention.   The Nineteenth century is studied much more intensively than the earlier periods.   Courses are also given in the Social Sciences. . By alternating the courses in both History and the Social Sciences each year it will be possible for the student to get a larger choice of courses than would be possible if the same instructors were compelled to repeat the courses each year.

History

1. Medieval.   Three Hours, First Semester.
From the Barbarian invasions to the Protestant Reformation.   The great forces and movements of Medieval history such as the Migrations and Founding of European nations, the Papacy.   Emphasis will be placed on social and economic institutions.   Such works as Thatcher and Schwill, Robinson, Emerton serve as a basis for the work.   Each student will be required to write a special term paper.   Not given 1918-19.

2. Modern.   Three Hours, Second Semester.
From the Protestant Reformation to the French Revolution. A study of the Reformation, the Counter Reformation, The Thirty-Year's War, The Ascendancy of France, Growth of Constitutionalism in England, Rise of Russia and Prussia. Schwill's Modern Europe will serve as a text with collateral reading.   Method of work same as History 1.   Not given 1918-19.

3. **English History.**   **Three Hours, First Semester.**
   From the beginning to the Revolution of 1688.   The
foundations of the English nation.   Special emphasis will be
placed on the institutional phases of the subject.   The study
will be based on a standard text.   Collateral reading and
special term reports will be required.

4. **English History.**   **Three Hours, Second Semester.**
   From the Revolution of 1688 to the present.   Text, collateral reading and reports as in Course 3.

5. **The French Revolution and Napoleonic Era.**
                              Two Hours, First Semester.
   A study of the causes, leading men, principal events and
permanent results of the Revolution, and the leading cam-
paigns, territorial changes and political, social and economic
results of the Napoleonic Era.   Bourne, Matthews, Rose,
Morse, Aulard and other texts furnish the reading for the
course.

6. **The Nineteenth Century.**   **Two Hours, Second Semester.**
   The great currents of Nineteenth Century history will
be studied.   The results of the French Revolution, the
Growth of Nationality, Rise of Democracy, the Eastern
Question and other subjects characteristic of the period will
be studied.   Special attention will be paid to the recent
Great War and the problems of current history.   Hazen's
Europe since 1815 will serve as a text.   Outside readnig and
special reports.

7. **American History.**   **Three Hours, First Semester.**
   From the beginning to 1812. The period covers the Early
Exploration, Founding of the Original Colonies, the Colonial Wars, the Revolution, the Founding of the Republic.
John Spencer Bassett will serve as a text with wide collateral reading in the leading authorities.   A teacher's course
giving special attention to methods in the grades.

8. **American History.**   **Three Hours, Second Semester.**
   From the second war with England to the present.   A
study of industrial development following the War of 1812.
Development of Internal Improvements, Rise of Slavery,
Civil War, Reconstruction, Recent economic and social

development. Texts, reading and reports the same as in Course 7.

21-22. Current History. One Hour, First and Sec. Semester.

A discussion of the current questions of the day, based on newspaper and magazine reading.

25-26. Teaching of History. One Hour, First and Sec. Semester.

A course in Methods of Teaching the subject, made up of lectures with assigned reading.

Government

9. American Government. Three Hours, First Semester.

A general study of the principal features of National, State and Municipal government. Special emphasis will be placed upon the practical working of government with special reference to current political problems. Such texts as Beard, Bryce, Ostrogorski will be used, together with reading from sources. Special reports.

10. European Government. Three Hours, Second Semester.

A comparative study of the National political systems of England, Germany, France, Italy, Austria, Switzerland and the Scandinavian countries with special reference to practical administration, manner of legislation and organization. Ogg, Wilson, Lowell will be used as a basis of work.

23. Elements of International Law. Two Hours, First Semester.

A study of the practises which in the past have controlled the relation of nations in their intercourse in war and peace. Special attention will be given to the source of international law and also the effect of the present war upon past practice. Not given in 1918-19.

24. American Political Theories. Two Hours, Second Semester.

The question will be taken up in its historical bearings. The various theories of the nature of our Federal government, held by publicists and statesmen, will be studied. Special attention will be given to the growth of Democracy and also to the relation of Federal to State Government. Not given in 1918-19.

Economics

13. The Elements of Economics.   Three Hours, First Semester.
A study of the fundamental principles underlying the general field of economic theory.   Based on a text with outside reading in source books and other available works of standard authors on the subject.   Not given 1918-19.

14. Economic Problems.   Three Hours, Second Semester.
This course deals with practical current economic problems springing out of our American industrial life and covers such questions as Taxation, Currency, Banknig, Wages, Labor Problems, Railroad Regulation, Industrial Organization, etc.   Not given 1918-1919.

15. Rural Economics.   Two Hours, First Semester.
This course takes up the history of agriculture, the problems of farm management, and such questions as co-operation in production, distribution and marketing, rural credit and other problems concerned with the economic welfare of the agricultural classes.   Lectures largely with collateral reading and class reports.

16. Taxation and Finance.   Two Hours, Second Semester.
A study of the principles which underlie the problems of public taxation and expenditure.   Much time will be devoted to the present conditions of State and Federal taxation, and a discussion of proposed methods for securing a more equitable distribution of our financial burdens.

Sociology

19. The Principles of Sociology.   Three Hours, First Semester.
A brief elementary course aiming to give a survey of the entire field of the science of Society.   The study includes a brief examination of the nature of social order, social evolution, the factors of social progress, the structure of society. A brief study will also be made of the most pressing social problems before our country, such as crime, poverty, effects of immigration, negro problem, and attention will also be paid to recent social legislation.

17. Social Legislation.   Two Hours, First Semester.
A survey of recent legislation on social and economic questions passed and proposed in various states.   Not given 1918-19.

18. Rural Sociology. **Three Hours, Second Semester.**

A discussion of the social problems of the open country, rural education, recreation, health, country church, and the various institutions and movements which are connected with a wholesome country life.

20. Socialism and Social Reform. Three Hrs., Second Semester.

This course covers the theory and history of early schemes for social reform from Plato to the present and includes a study of communism and anarchism. Present socialism in Europe and America will be studied both from the great writers on the subject as well as from contemporary and current literature. The work will be largely in the form of lectures with outside reading. Not given 1918-19.

IX. HOME ECONOMICS
* Miss Streid
Miss Boehr

The courses in this department are planned to meet the needs of two classes of students:

(1)   Those who are specializing in other lines of study and desire some knowledge of Home Economics as part of a general education.

(2)   Those students who desire a special study of Home Economics necessary for teaching the subject in the public schools, or for the profession of home-keeper.

Students may major in this department following the full four year course leading to the A. B. degree as outlined below. The requirements for admission are the same as those for other college courses.

Four-Year Course
FRESHMEN

First Semester	Hrs.	Second Semester	Hrs.
English 1	2	English 2	2
Mathematics 3	3	Mathematics 3	3
Chemistry 1	4	Chemistry 2	4
Sewing 7	3	Advanced Sewing 6	3
Textiles 5	2	Design	2
Drawing	1	Drawing	1

* Absent on leave.

SOPHOMORE

First Semester		Second Semester	
English 5	3	English 6	3
Modern Language	4	Modern Language	4
Chemistry 3	3	House Sanitation 8	2
General Biology	3	General Biology	3
Food and Its Preparation 1	3	Food and Its Preparation 2	3

JUNIOR

First Semester		Second Semester	
		Modern Language	4
Modern Language	4	Physiology 7	3
Bacteriology 8	3	Food and Dieteics 4	3
Chemistry 7	3	Bible	2
Bible	2	Household Management 10	3
House Furnishing 9	2		

SENIOR

First Semester		Second Semester	
History	3	History	3
Sociology	3	Observation and Practice.	3
Teach. of Home Economics 11	2	Electives	9
Electives	7		

1-2. **Food and Its Preparation.** Three Hours, Two Semesters.
The study of foods including food production and manufacture. Emphasis is placed on methods of preparation and the influence of these methods on the structure and general composition of foods. The preparation and serving of breakfasts, luncheons and dinners.

Prerequisite Chemistry 1. One recitation and two laboratory periods a week.

4. **Food and Dietetics.** Three Hours, Second Semester.
The purpose of this course is to present the fundamental principles of human nutrition and their application under varying physiological and economic conditions. Typical dietaries are planned.

Prerequisite Home Economics 1-2. One recitation and two laboratory periods a week.

3. Design. **Two Hours, Second Semester.**

A course including a discussion of the elements of design and color. Conventionalized nature forms designs for stencil work and interior decorations are worked.

5. Textiles. **Two Hours, First Semester.**

This course is the study of the various textile fibers, the development of spinning, weaving, modern processes of manufacture, and the comparison of textile fabrics with special reference to suitability to use and value to the consumer.

One recitation and one laboratory period a week.

7. Sewing. **Three Hours, First Semester.**

This course is based on the fundamental principles underlying the construction of garments. Introduces drafting and construction of undergarments. Both hand and machine sewing are used.

One recitation and two laboratory periods a week.

6. Advanced Sewing. **Three Hours, Second Semester.**

This course offers more technical work in clothing with emphasis on the principles of construction underlying elementary dress-making. History of costume and the study of color and design in relation to clothing is taken up.

Prerequisite, Design and Home Economics 7. One recitation and two laboratory periods a week.

8. House Sanitation. **Two Hours, Second Semester.**

This course deals with the house as a factor in health. Location and construction of the house from the point of view of sanitation, water supply, plumbing, heating, ventilating, and lighting.

9. House Furnishing. **Two Hours, First Semester.**

A study of line, mass, and color as used in house decoration including such phases as the treatment of walls, floors and windows in relation to color schemes, fabrics and expense.

Prerequisite, Design.

10. Household Management. **Three Hours, Second Semester.**

This course aims to give the principles underlying housekeeping, including the organization of the household, the family income and its expenditures, methods of buying household supplies, and the care of the home.

11. **Teaching of Home Economics. Two Hours, First Semester.**

This course considers the problem of Home Economics in the elementary and secondary schools. It includes the arrangement of courses of study, discussion of the method of presentation of subject matter, and the problem of equipping laboratories.

X. MATHEMATICS AND ASTRONOMY
Professor Hirschler

The courses in this department are arranged to meet the needs of four classes of students, as follows: (1) Those who wish to study Mathematics for general culture. (2) Those who wish to take Mathematics in preparation for advanced work in other departments. (3) Those who wish to become teachers of Mathematics in secondary schools. (4) Those who wish to specialize in Mathematics in preparation for research work or the teaching of the Higher Mathematics. The courses offered may be divided into an elementary group and an advanced group, the first comprising courses 1-8 in Pure Mathematics and courses 21-22 in Astronomy. The courses required of Freshmen are any two of courses 1-4 for which they are prepared. Students of the first two classes mentioned above would be greatly benefited by taking in addition to the required courses numbers 5-8. Students who intend to teach Mathematics in high schools should take all of the courses of group one, and a sufficient number of additional courses including course 15, to make a major. Those who intend to specialize in Mathematics should take courses 1-8 and then consult the head of the department for further direction.

Mathematics

1. Algebra. Four Hours, First Semester.

A review of Elementary Algebra; radicals, exponents, including fractional and negative, quadratic equations in one and two unknown quantities; problems leading to quadratics; graphical solution of quadratic systems; progressions; ratio, proportion and variation; binomial theorem; logarithms.

2. Solid Geometry.   **Four Hours, Second Semester.**

The relations of planes and lines in space; properties and measurement of prisms, pyramids, cylinders and cones; the sphere and the spherical triangle; numerous original exercises including applications to the mensuration of surfaces and solids.

3. College Algebra.   **Three Hours, First Semester.**

Rapid review of elementary algebra; functions and graphical representation; complex numbers; elements of the theory of equations including Horner's method of approximation; permutations and combinations; determinants; logarithms.

4. Plane Trigonometry.   **Three Hours, Second Semester.**

The six trigonometric functions; principal formulas of plane trigonometry and the transformation of trigonometric expressions by means of these formulas; the solution of trigonometric equations; the solution of right and oblique triangles and applications.

5. Analytical Geometry I.   **Two Hours, First Semester.**

Cartesian co-ordinates; loci and their equations; lengths, areas; the straight line; the circle; elements of the parabola, the ellipse and the hyperbola.

6. Analytical Geometry II.   **Two Hours, Second Semester.**

Conic sections; transformation of co-ordinates; polar co-ordinates; higher plane curves; parametric equations; tangents and normals.

7. Calculus I.   **Three Hours, First Semester.**

Must be preceded or accompanied by course 5. Prerequisites, courses 3 and 4. Differential calculus; fundamental principles; derivatives; applications to geometry and mechanics; maxima and minima; indeterminates.

8. Calculus II.   **Three Hours, Second Semester.**

Prerequisites, courses 5 and 7. May be taken at the same time with course 6. Integral calculus; integration; definite integrals; applications to lengths, areas and volumes.

9. **Calculus III.**   **Three Hours, First Semester.**
Applications of the calculus to curves and surfaces; series; partial differentiation; partial integration and applications to areas and volumes; multiple integrals; approximate integration; and a thorough training in the use of a definite integral as a sum. Not given 1918-19.

10. **Differential Equations.**   **Three Hours, Second Semester.**
Prerequisites, courses 3 to 8. Ordinary differential equations; special forms of differential equations of higher order; integration in series; partial differential equations; applications to geometry and physics. Not given 1918-19.

11. **Solid Analytical Geometry.**   **Two Hours, First Semester.**
Prerequisites, courses 5 to 8. May be conveniently taken at the same time with course 9. Equations of the plane and right line in space; the more general properties of surfaces of the second degree; the classification and special properties of quadric surfaces.

12. **History of Mathematics.**   **Two Hours, Second Semester.**
Prerequisites, courses 3 to 8. Historical development of the elementary subjects; rise and growth of higher mathematics, chiefly during the nineteenth century; biography of the persons most influential in its development.
Recitations, reports on assigned readings. Not given 1918-19.

13. **Theory of Equations and Determinants.**
                         Three Hours, First Semester.
A study of the general equation of the second and higher degrees; the solution of the cubic and biquadratic; separation of the roots of an equation including Sturm's Theorem; the solution of numerical equations; some fundamental properties of determinants; the solution of systems of linear equations.

14. **Higher Algebra.**   **Three Hours, Second Semester.**
The development of the number system of Algebra; definition of irrational number; fundamental theorems on limits; convergence of infinite series; binomial, exponential and logarithmic series; power series; infinite products; properties of continuous functions; the fundamental theorem of Algebra.

16. The Teaching of Mathematics.

Three Hours, Second Semester

A study of the values, aims and methods of mathematical teaching wiht special reference to the topics usually taught in secondary schools. The most important topics of elementary Algebra and Geometry are given special attention.

Astronomy

21-22. General Astronomy.

Two hours throughout the year with occasional evenings for observation.

Prerequisite, course 4. This is a general course mainly descriptive in character. It sets forth the leading facts of Astronomy and gives an elementary explanation of the methods by which they are ascertained. Not given 1918-19.

XI. MODERN LANGUAGES
Professor Thierstein
Miss Mueller
French

The purpose of the courses in French is to give the student a fair reading, writing, and some speaking knowledge of the language, thus bringing him in touch with an interesting people, rich in thought, in literary treasure, culture and refinement.

1-2. Elementary French.   Four Hours, Two Semesters.

A mastery of the essentials of grammar, with particular attention to principles of pronunciation and verb-drills. Reading and translating easy prose selections, such as "La Tache du Petit Pierre," etc., memorizing idioms, dictation exercises, conversation. Written and oral work in composition.

3. Second Year French.   Four Hours, First Semester.

Grammar completed. Dictation. Theme writing in French. Extensive reading and some translating of such literature as "Ca et La en France," "La Neuvaine de Colette," "Columba," etc.

4. Second Year French.   Four Hours, Second Semester.

Reading of modern prose authors. Written resumes of books read. Composition work. Dictation exercises.

5. Corneille and Racine.   Two Hours, First Semester.

After a brief survey of the entire field of French literature, particular attention will be given to the great dram-
atists of the seventeenth century.   Special study of Corneille and Racine. Reading of several tragedies of each
writer.   Composition and conservation.   Reports on assigned topics.   Open to students who have completed
French 4.

6. Moliere.   Two Hours, Second Semester.

A study of the life and comedies of Moliere, with written
and oral resumes.   Open to students who have completed
French 5.

7. The Romantic School.   Two Hours, First Semester.

A study of the literature of the romantic period, with
readings from representative writers of the period.   Not
given 1918-19.

8. Nineteenth Century Literature.
**   Two Hours, Second Semester**

A study of the prose and poetry of this period, with
readings from representatives authors. Not given 1918-19.

German

Courses are arranged with these ends in view: To train
the student to speak German; to lead him to know and appre-
ciate the literature, life and art of the German people; to prepare him to be a thoroughly efficient teacher of German, if this
be his aim.

At least four years of German, counting two years of high
school German as one, are required of students who desire the
recommendation of the department for teachers of German in
high schools.

"I do not think our present relations with the German Em-
pire should affect in any way the policy of the schools in the
United States in regard to the teaching of the German Language."—Hon P. P. Claxton, U. S. Com. Ed.

11-12. Elementary German. **Four Hours, Two Semesters.**

A thorough study of the fundamentals of the language, constant drill in pronunciation, and acquisition of a simple, usable vocabulary; easy narrative prose, with conservation upon the same; paraphrasing and translation when necessary.

13. Second Year German. **Four Hours, First Semester.**

Continued study of grammar and syntax; systematic composition and conversation. Literature: Modern prose from such authors as Heyse, Storm, Keller, Rosegger and Meyer. One classic read outside.

14. Second Year German. **Four Hours, Second Semester.**

Grammatical study, composition and conservation as above. Literature: Schiller's Wilhelm Tell and Lessing's Minna von Barnhelm in class. Another classic read outside.

15. Select German Prose. **Three Hours, First Semester.**

Study of representative novels, such as Freytag's Soll und Haben, Sudermann's Frau Sorge, Frenssen's Joern Uhl, Ludwig's Zwischen Himmel und Erde or others. Heine's Harzreise or Metzger und Mueller's Kreuz und Quer durch deutsche Lande for outside reading. German themes.

16. Classic German Poetry. **Three Hours, Second Semester.**

A brief survey of the leading periods of later German poetry. Study of popular lyrics and ballads. Schiller's die Jungfrau von Orleans and Goethe's Hermann und Dorothea. German themes.

17-18. Intermediate German Composition.

One Hour, Two Semesters.

Exercises in composition and in the use of idioms, with all needed review in grammar. This course is to be taken in connection with courses 15 and 16. Credit for entire course only.

19. Lessing. **Three Hours, First Semester.**

Lessing's life, works and significance in German thought and literature. Rapid reading of minor dramas. Essentials of der Laokoon und die Hamburger Dramaturgie. Careful study of Emilia Galotti and Nathan der Weise. German themes. Not given 1918-19.

20. Schiller.   Three Hours, Second Semester.

Schiller's life and works.   Introductory to this, a study of the Sturm und Drangperiode; its cause and significance, as exemplified in Schiller's early dramas.   Study of several dramas, including Wallenstein. German themes. Not given 1918-19.

21-22. Goethe.   Two Hours, Two Semesters.

Goethe's life and works.   His place and significance in German and universal literature. Study of Dichtung und Wahrheit, Goetz von Berlichingen, Iphigenie, and one other productions.   Second semester, all of Faust.   German themes.

23. Lyrics and Ballads.   Three Hours, First Semester.

Study of the Minnesang, Volkslied, Geistliche Lieder of Gerhardt, Fleming, Spee, Luther, Gellert, Novalis, Knapp, Spitta, Gerok and others.   Lyric and ballad poetry of Buerger, Goethe, Schiller, the Romanticists and later poets. Themes. Offered summer 1918.

24. Modern German Drama.   Three Hours, Second Semester.

Study of selected dramas of Kleist and Grillparzer, Hebbel, Ludwig, Anzengruber and Wildenbruch, Hauptmann and Sudermann, together with the types and tendencies of each. Themes. Offered summerr 1918.

25. History of German Literature. Three Hours, Two Semesters.

A systematic study of German literature from the earliest times, giving special attention to the origin, growth and influence of the chief literary movements. Typical productions of authors or periods are read.   A simple text like Klee's or Kluge's in the hands of the student, with constant reference to Scherer's, Biese's, Koenig's, and Vogt's and Koch's Geschichten der deutschen Literatur, and lectures by the instructor.

27. Advanced German Composition. Three Hrs., First Semester.

Review of the more difficult portions of grammar, with exercises illustrating each. Study of and weekly exercises in narrative, descriptive and expository composition; also translations from English texts.

28. **Teachers' Course in German.** Three Hrs., Second Semester.

Study of the teachers' work and problems in high school German. Methods are studied and illustrated, text-books, works of reference and other helps considered, and the more difficult phases of grammar, phonetics and pronunciation, etc., are taken up in review.

Spanish

31-32. **Elementary Spanish.** Four Hours, Two Semesters.

Mastery of elements of grammar. Special emphasis is placed on pronunciation and vocabulary. Reading of simple texts. Composition and conservation.

33-34. **Second Year Spanish.** Four Hours, Two Semesters.

Advanced grammar. Composition and readings from Alacron, Galdos, Valdes, Valera and others. Conversation and composition. Increased use of Spanish in classroom. Not given 1918-19.

XII. MUSIC

Assistant Professor Lehmann

The following studies in Music may be applied to the degree of Bachelor of Arts:

Appreciation of Music 1-2; Chorus and Choir Training 5; Church Music 6; Composition Counterpoint 7-8; Form and Analysic 11-12; Harmony 13-16, inclusive; History of Music 17-20; Public School Music Methods 22, inclusive. Practic Music to the extent of eight hours upon the following conditions:

(a) Student must have completed the following Theory Courses—Harmony 13-16; Counterpoint 7-8; History 17-20.

(b) The number of hours credit will be determined by the number of compositions studied in the various courses. A list of the works studied must be presented.

(c) The work of student shall be recommended by his teacher of practical music as having attained sufficient advancement to warrant College credit. Not more than twenty-four hours of Music can be counted toward A. B. degree unless student pursues the Literary-Music Course of the Conservatory. Description of these courses will be found under the outline of Conservatory Courses.

XIII. PHILOSOPHY

Professor Byers

The purpose of the courses in Psychology is to help the student to understand his own mental activities, to acquaint him with the laws of mental growth, and to give him the power of applying this knowledge to the work of teaching and other vocations.

The courses in Philosophy aim to give the student a knowledge of the development of the philosophical thought and to aid him to think in a thorough-going manner with reference to the fundamental problems of life as a basis for true living.

Students expecting to major in this department should take General Psychology during their Sophomore year; others are not expected to take their electives in these subjects earlier than the Junior year.

Psychology

1. General Psychology.   Three Hours, First Semester.
   After a brief survey of the general field of the subject, the course is devoted entirely to normal human psychology. The genetic and functional viewpoints are emphasized. Angell and James are used as texts, supplemented by demonstrations and lectures.

2. Experimental Psychology.   Three Hours, Second Semester.
   This is a laboratory course, giving training in experimental methods and an introduction to the chief results of experimental psychology. Sensation and perception in the different sense fields, attention, association and other higher mental processes are included. Not given 1918-19.

3. Child Psychology.   Three Hours, First Semester.
   The characteristics of the different periods of childhood and youth are studied. Special attention is given to the study of the instincts and the means by which they may be developed into useful reactions or serve as a starting point for mental development.

4. Educational Psychology.   Three Hours, Second Semester.
   A study of the psychological basis of the educative process. Special attention will be given to such topics as laws

of learning, interest, attention, appreciation, memory, habits and mental measurements, considered with special reference to the work of the teacher. Text-book, experiments and supplementary reading.

5. Applied Psychology.   Three Hours, First Semester.
Following a brief survey of general psychology a study is made of its application to the professions of law and medicine, to the business world and to public speaking. Prerequisite, Elementary Psychology.

7. Psychology of Religion.   Two Hours, First Semester.
A psychological study of religious experience. Special attention is given to the study of the adolescent period and the psychology of conversion. A critical study is made of the literature of the subject.

Philosophy

8. Ethics.   Three Hours, Second Semester.
A critical and comparative study is made of the leading schools of ethics, followed by the formulation of a theory of the moral life, and its application to modern, social and economic problems. Wide reading of texts and the works of leading ethical philosophers, lectures and theses.

9. Logic   Three Hours, First Semester.
A study of deductive and inductive reasoning and a brief discussion of the nature of thought. Much exercise is given in the examination of argument and the detection of fallacies. Not given 1918-19.

10. Introduction to Philosophy.   Three Hrs. Second Semester.
A general survey of the field and problems of philosophy. The ultimate nature of mind and its relation to matter, the problems of philosophy, the problems of knowledge and being and the classification of the chief schools of thought are discussed. Prerequisites, Philosophy 1 and 9. Not given 1918-19.

11-12. History of Philosophy.   Three Hours, Two Semesters.
This course will include a study of the development of constructive thought from the beginning of Greek philosophy to the present time. At the close of the course a brief summary will be given of the present philosophic positions.

The text-books will be supplanted by extensive reading of the most important philosophers. Prerequisite, one year's work in Philosophy.

14. Philosophy of Religion.   Three Hours, Second Semester.
This is a study of the fundamental principles of religion as related to philosophy and science and seeks to aid the student in acquiring freedom in critical thinking, and in gaining a unified view of the world in which religious truth and life find their proper place.

16. Aesthetics.   Three Hours, Second Semester.
A study of the nature and elements of our aesthetic judgment. The method is psychological in that the facts of feeling with reference to our standards, judgements, and expression of the beautiful are studied. Prerequisite, Elementary Psychology.

17. Modern Idealism.   Three Hours, First Semester.
This is a course in Metaphysics based on Royce's The World and The Individual. Ie serves as a good introduction to the Philosophy of Religion. Prerequisite, one year of Philosophy. Not given in 1918-19.

18. Contemporary Philosophy. Three Hours, Second Semester.
This is a study of some of the most important movements in contemporary thought. Special attention will be given to James, Eucken and Bergson. Prerequisite, one year of Philosophy. Not given in 1918-19.

XIV. PHYSICAL SCIENCES

Assistant Professor Berky

Mr. Pannebecker

The aim of the courses in the Physical Sciences is to give the student in his first year a brief general idea of the organization and relation of the inanimate world and to stimulate interest in scientific work. At the same time an effort is made to become acquainted with some of the world's greatest scientists.

The subsequent courses are more or less special, in which we strive to give the student a working knowledge of scientific laws, and a realm of exact reasoning; to make him more proficient, in the use of instruments of precision and more exact and painstaking in his methods.

The aim of these courses is two-fold: First, to present and emphasize the great scientific problems of the day and thus stimulate a desire for research work; second, to prepare the student for educational work.

Chemistry

1-2. General Inorganic Chemistry. Four Hours, Two Semesters.

Experimental lectures, recitations and quizzes on the elements and their compounds, supplemented by laboratory work. Two lectures and recitations a week and two laboratory periods. The laboratory work is in part introductory to qualitative analysis. Smith's General Chemistry for College.

3-4. Qualitative Analysis.   Three Hours, Two Semesters.

The chemistry of the more important metals accompanied by the preparation of a number of inorganic compounds and the study and practice of the methods of separating and detectingfi followed by the analysis of simple and complex substances. This course involves 6 to 8 hours of laboratory work, beside class room exercises each week.

Prerequisite course: General Chemistry.

Note: Students majoring in Home Economics may take Qualitative Analysis (3), first semester.

5-6. Quantitative Analysis.   Three Hours, Two Semesters.

The theory and practice of typical gravimetric and volumetric analysis, chiefly analysis of simple salts during first term. Second term, salts, minerals, alloys, etc. This course involves from 9 to 10 hours of laboratory work in addition to one or more class exercises each week. Junior or Senior course. Prerequisite courses: General Chemistry and Qualitative Analysis. Not given 1918-19.

7-8. Organic Chemistry.   Three Hours, Two Semesters.

Lectures, recitations on the chemistry of the typical compounds of carbon, supplemented by laboratory work. Determination of specific gravities, melting and boiling points, vapor densities. Preparation of organic compounds, examination of food stuffs.   Two lectures and two laboratory periods a week. Prerequisite courses: General Chemistry and Qualitative Analysis.

Note: Students majoring in Home Economics may take Organic Chemistry (7), first semester. Experiments, especially adapted to the needs of such students, have been arranged for.

9-10. General College Physics.   **Four Hours, Two** Semesters.

General course in Physics, including lectures, recitation, laboratory work, and class room demonstrations. Mechanics, sound, light, heat, electricity, and magnetism.

XV. PHYSICAL TRAINING

Mr. Oliver M. Kratz, Director

Miss Alice Mueller, Assistant

1. Hygiene.   One **Hour, Two Semesters.**

All Freshmen are required to attend lectures on personal hygiene every other week during the year.

2. Physical Training.   **Two Hours, Two Semesters.**

All Freshmen are required to take two hours per week of systematic training in the gymnasium. Candidates for the A. B. degree are required to complete six hours of this training.

EXPENSES

ALL TUITION AND FEES are payable in advance, by the semester. All bills are made out by the Business Manager of the college and the amounts paid to him.

Tuition, including incidental fees, per semester:

College $35.00
Preparatory 25.00

A rebate of $2 per semester or $5 per year is given if tuition paid within ten days after registration day.

Physics, yearly deposit for breakage 1.00
Physics Fee, per semester 3.00
Biology Fee, per semester 3.00
Chemistry, yearly deposit for breakage.......... 5.00
Chemistry Fee, per semester 5.00
Home Economics Fee, per semester ....2.50 to 5.00
Oratory, class work, per semester.............. 5.00
Oratory, private lessons, per smeester 15.00
Art, one course, per semester ....5.00 to 9.00

Students in College taking more than sixteen hours of regular work will be charged extra tuition at the rate of $2.00 per semester hour.

Students doing preparatory work can take eighteen hours of regular work without extra tuition. For all extra hours of work they will be charged $1.50 per semester hour.

Any student who takes two courses or less in the College will be charged tuition at the rate of $2.00 per semester hour. Preparatory students will pay at the rate of $1.50 a semester hour.

Students registered in the preparatory department will be charged College rates for College work and students registered in the College, but doing preparatory work, will be charged preparatory rates for the work they do in that department.

A diploma fee of $5.00 is charged for diplomas granted in any course and a fee of $2.00 for certificates. This fee, must be paid to the Business Manager of the College not later than Thursday preceding commencement week.

SCHEDULE OF RECITATIONS—FIRST SEMESTER

Hours	TUESDAY	WEDNESDAY	THURSDAY	FRIDAY	SATURDAY
7:45	El. French (M.L. 1) 2nd yr. Ger. (M.L.13) Child Psychol (P. 3) Church Music (Mu. 6) Eng. Hist. (H. 3) Novel Course (E. 13)	El. French (M.L.1) 2nd yr. Ger. (M.L.13) Ele Greek (A.L.1) Botany (B.S.3) Algebra (M.1) Chr. Ethics (S.Th.3) Pub. Speaking (E.15) Col. Physics (P.S.9) Rhetoric (E.3)	El. French (M.L.1) 2nd yr. Ger. (M.L.13) Ele. Greek (A.L.1) Child Psychol. (P.3) Algebra (M.1) Church Music (Mu.6) Eng. Hist. (H.3) Col. Physics (P.S.9) Novel Course (E.13)	El. French (M.L.1) 2nd yr. Ger. (M.L.13) Ele. Greek (A.L.1) Botany (B.S.3) Algebra (M.1) Chr. Ethics (S.Th.3) Pub. Speak. (E.15) Col. Physics (P.S.9) Rhetoric (E.3)	El. Greek (A.L.1) Child Psychol. (P.3) Algebra (M.1) Church Music (Mu.6) Eng. History (H.3) Col. Physics (P.S.9)
8:40	2nd yr. French(M.L.3) Amer. History (H. 7) Col. Algebra (M. 3) Second Ed. (Ed. 5) Cicero (A.L.15) Mod. Prob. O.T.(B.13) Harmony (Mu. 15) Biology (B. S. 1)	2nd yr. French (M.L.3) Botany (B.S.3) Cicero (A.L.15) Pentateuch (B.5) Design (H.E.3)	2nd yr. French (M.L.3) Amer. Hist. (H.7) Col. Algebra (M.3) Second Ed. (Ed.5) Cicero (A.L.15) Mod. Prob.O.T.(B.13) Col. Physics (P.S.9) Biology (B.S.1)	2nd yr. French M.L.3) Botany (B.S.3) Cicero (A.L.15) Pentateuch (B.5) Harmony (Mu. 15) Design (H.E.3)	Amer. History (H.7) Col. Algebra (M.3) Second Ed. (Ed.5) Col. Physics (P.S.9) Biology (B.S.1)
9:35	Cicero (A.L. 11) Sociology (H. 19) Hist. of Ed. (Ed. 1) Lessing (H. L. 19) Calculus (M. 7) Hist. of Music (Mu.17) Biology (B. S. 1)	El. Germ. (M.L.11) Cicero (A.L.11) Rural School (Ed.7) Botany (B.S.3) Composition (E.1) Analytics (M.5) Design (H.E.3) Harmony (Mu.13)	El. Germ. (M.L.11) Cicero (A.L.11) Sociology (H.19) Hist. of Ed. (Ed. 1) Calculus (M.7) Biology (B.S.1)	El. Germ. (M.L.11) Cicero (A.L.11) Rural Econ. (H.15) Rural School (Ed.7) Botany (B.S.3) Composition (E.1) Analytics (M.5) Design (H.E.3) Hist. of Mu. (Mu.17)	El. Germ. (M.L.11) Sociology (H.19) History of Ed. (Ed.1) Calculus (M.7) Textiles (H.E.5) Biology (B.S.1)
10:30	Chapel	Chapel	Chapel	Chapel.	

Hours	TUESDAY	WEDNESDAY	THURSDAY	FRIDAY	SATURDAY
10:50	English Lit. (E. 5) Ger. Prose (M. L. 15) Hist. of Phil. (P. 11) Am. Govern't (H.9) House Furn. (H. E. 9)	Composition (E.1) Goethe (M.L.21) Psychol of Rel. (P.7) Current Hist. (H.21) Solid Analytics (M.11) N. T. Lit. (B.11) Teach H. E. (H.E.11)	English Lit. (E.5) Germ. Prose (M.L.15) Hist. of Phil. (P.11) Am. Govern't (H.9) House Furn. (H.E.9)	Composition (E.1) Psychol. of Rel. (P.7) Goethe (M.L.21) Teaching Hist. (H.25) Solid Analytics (M11) N. T. Lit. (B.11) Teach H. E. (H.E.11)	English Lit. (E.5) Germ. Prose (M.L.15) Hist. of Phil. (P.11) Am. Governm't (H.9)
1:00	Gen. Chemistry (P.S.1) Ap. Psy. (P. 5) Hist. Ger. Lit. (M.L.25) Amer. Lit. (E.7) Appreciation (Mu. 1) Sewing (H.E.7) Agriculture (A. 1)	Zoology (B.S.5) Corn.& Racine (M.L.5) Qual. Anal. (P.S.5) Prep. of Foods (H.E.1)	Gen. Chemist. (P.S.1) Ap. Psychol. (P.5) Hist. Ger. Lit. (M.L.25) Amer. Lit. (E.7) Sewing (H.E.7) Agriculture (A.1)	Zoology (B.S.5) Corn.& Racine (M.L.5) Qual. Anal. (P.S.5) Harmony (Mu. 13) Prep. of Foods (H.E.1)	Ap. Psychol. (P.5) Hist. Ger. Lit. (M.L.25) Amer. Lit. (E.7) Textiles (H. E. 5) Agriculture (A.1)
2:00	Gen. Chemist. (P.S.1) Bacteriology (B.S.7) 19th Cent. Poet. (E.9) Hist. of Mu. (Mu.19) Sewing (H.E.7)	Zoology (B.S.5) Gen. Psychol. (P.1) Qual. Anal. (P.S.5) Prep. of Foods (H.E.1) Ele . Spanish (M.L.31)	Gen. Chemist. (P.S.1) Bacteriology (B.S.7) 19th Cent. Poet. (E.9) Sewing (H.E.7) Ele . Spanish (M.L.31)	Zoology (B.S.5) Gen. Psychol. (P.1) Qual. Anal. (P.S.5) Hist. of Mu. (Mu.19) Prep. of Foods (H.E.1) Ele. Spanish (M.L.32)	Gen. Psychol. (P.1) Bacteriology (B.S.7) 19th Cent. Poet. (E.9) Textiles (H.E.5) Ele. Spanish (M.L.31)
3:00	Gen. Chemist. (P.S.1) Methods (Ed. 3) Ad. Ger. Co. (M.L.27) Bible in Lit. (C.H.13) Sewing (H.E.7)	Zoology (B.S.5) Qual. Anal. (P.S.5) Solfeggio (Mu.23) Prep. of Foods (H.E.1)	Gen. Chemist. (P.S.1) Methods (Ed. 3) Ad. Ger. Co. (M.L.27) Bible in Lit. (C.H.13)	Zoology (B.S.5) Qual. Anal. (P.S.5) Analysis (Mu.12)	Ad. Ger. Co. (M.L.27) Methods (Ed.3) Bible in Lit. (C.H.13)

SCHEDULE OF RECITATIONS—SECOND SEMESTER

Hours	TUESDAY	WEDNESDAY	THURSDAY	FRIDAY	SATURDAY
7:45	El. French (M.L.2) 2nd yr. Ger. (M.L.14) Ed. Psychol. (P.4) Eng. Hist. (H.4) House Mgt. (H.E.10) Novel Course (E14)	El. French (M.L.2) 2nd yr. Ger. (M.L.14) El. Greek (A.L.2) Pub. Sch. Mu. (Mu.22) Botany (B.S.4) Solid Geom. (M.2) Chr. Ethics (S.Th.4) Debating (E.16) Col. Physics (P.S.10) Rhetoric (E.4)	El. French (M.L.2) 2nd yr. Ger. (M.L.14) El. Greek (A.L.2) Solid Geom. (M.2) Ed. Psychology (P.4) Eng. Hist. (H.4) House Mgt (H.E.10) Col. Physics (P.S.10) Novel Course (E.14)	El. French (M.L.2) 2nd yr. Ger. (M.L.14) El. Greek (A.L.2) Botany (B.S.4) Solid Geom. (M.2) Chr. Ethics (S.Th.4) Pub. Sch. Mu. (Mu.22) Debating (E.16) Col. Physics (P.S.10) Rhetoric (E.4)	El. Greek (A.L.2) Ed. Psychol. (P.4) Solid Geom. (M.2) Eng. Hist. (H.4) House Mgt. (H.E.10) Col. Physics (P.S.10)
8:40	2nd yr. French (M.L.4) Amer. History (H.7) Trigonometry (M.4) Horace (A.L.16) Mod. Prob. O.T.(B.14) Harmony Mu.16 Sewing (H.E.6) Biology (B.S.2)	2nd yr. French (M.L.4) Horace (A.L.16) Prophecy (B.6) Botany (B.S.4) Sewing (H.E.6)	2nd yr. French (M.L.4) Amer. History (H.7) Trigonometry (M.4) Horace (A.L.16) Mod. Prob. O.T. (B.14) Col. Physics (P.S.10) Sanitation (H.E.8) Biology (B.S.2)	2nd yr. French (M.L.4) Prophecy (B.6) Botany (B.S.4) Horace (A.L.16) Harmony (Mu.16) Sewing (H.E.6)	Amer. Hist. (H.7) Trigonometry (M.4) Col. Physics (P.S.10) Sanitation (H.E.8) Biology (B.S.2)
9:35	Cicero (A.L.12) Rural Soc. (H.18) Calculus (M.8) Ed. Theory (Ed.2) Hist. of Mu. (Mu.18) Biology (B.S.2)	El. Ger. (M.L.12) Cicero (A.L.12) Taxation (H.16) Botany (B.S.4) Analytics (M.6) Ed. Classics (Ed.6) Composition (E.2) Harmony (Mu.14)	El. Ger. (M.L.12) Cicero (A.L.12) Rural Soc. (H.18) Calculus (M.8) Ed. Theory (Ed.2) Sewing (H.E.6) Biology (B.S.2)	El. Ger. (M.L.12) Cicero (A.L.12) Taxation (H.16) Botany (B.S.4) Analytics (M.6) Composition (E.2) Ed. Classics (Ed.6) Hist. of Mu. (Mu.18) Sewing (H.E.6)	El. Ger. (M.L.12) Rural Soc. (H.18) Calculus (M.8) Ed. Theory (E.2) Biology (B.S.2)
10:30	Chapel	Chapel	Chapel	Chapel	Chapel

Hours	TUESDAY	WEDNESDAY	THURSDAY	FRIDAY	SATURDAY
10:50	English Lit. (E.6) Ger. Poetry (M.L.16) Hist. of Philos. (P.12) Eu, Governm't (H.10)	Composition (E.2) Goethe (M.L.21) Ed. Measurm. (Ed.14) Philos. of Rel. (P.14) N. T. Lit. (B.12) Current Hist. (H.22) Hist. of Math. (M.12)	English Lit. (E.6) Ger. Poetry (M.L.16) Hist. of Philos. (P.12) Eu. Governm't (H.10) Gen. Chemis. (P.S.2)	Composition (E.2) Goethe (M.L.21) Ed. Measurm. (Ed.14) Philos. of Rel. (P.14) N. T. Lit. (B.12) Teach. History (H.26) Hist. of Math. (M.12)	English Lit. (E.6) Ger. Poetry (M.L.16) Hist. of Philos. (P.12) Eu. Governm't (H.10)
1:00	Gen. Chemis. (P.S.2) Aesthetics (P.16) Hist. Ger. Lit. (M.L.26) Teach. Agricult. (A.2) Amer. Lit. (H.8) Appreciation (Mu.2) Food & Dietet (H.E.4)	Zoology (B.S.6) Qual. Anal. (P.S.6) 19 Cent.Fr.Lit.(M.L.8) Teach. Latin (A.L.23) Uses of Foods (H.E.2)	Aesthetics (P.16) Hist. Ger.Lit. (M.L.26) Teach. Agricult. (A.2) Amer. Lit. (H.8)	Zoology (B.S.6) Qual. Anal. (P.S.6) 19 Cent.Fr.Lit.(M.L.8) Teach. Latin (A.L.24) Harmony (Mu.1) Uses of Foods (H.E.2)	Aesthetics (P.16) Hist. Ger. Lit. (M.L.26) Teach. Agricult. (A.2) Amer. Lit. (H.8)
2:00	Gen. Chemis. (P.S.2) Physiology (B.S.10) 19th Cent.Poetry(E.10) Hist. of Mu. (Mu.20) Food & Dietet (H.E.4)	Zoology (B.S.6) Ethics (P.2) Qual. Anal. (P.S.6) Uses of Foods (H.E.2) Ele. Spanish (M.L.32)	Gen. Chemis. (P.S.2) Food & Dietet (H.E.4) Physiology (B.S.10) 19th Cent.Poetry(E.10) Food & Dietet (H.E.4) Ele. Spanish (M.L.32)	Zoology (B. S. 6) Ethics (P.2) Qual. Anal. (P.S.6) Hist. of Mu. (Mu. 20) Uses of Foods (H.E.2) Ele. Spanish M.L.32)	Ethics (P.2) Physiology (B.S.10) 19th Cent.Poetry(E.10) Ele. Spanish (M.L.32)
3:00	Gen. Chemis. P.S.2) School Admin. (Ed. 8) Food & Dietet (H.E.4) Conducting (Mu.5) Tch. C. in Ger(M.L.28) Bible in Lit. (C.H.14)	Zoology (B.S.6) School Mang't (Ed.4) Qual. Anal. (P.S.6) Solfeggio (Mu. 24) Uses of Foods (H.E.2)	Gen. Chemis. (P.S.2) School Admin. (Ed.8) Tch. C. in Ger. (ML28) Conducting (Mu.5) Bible in Lit. (C.H.13)	Zoology (B.S.6) School Mang't (Ed.4) Qual. Anal. (P.S.6) Analysis (Mu.12)	Tch. C. in Ger.(ML28) Bible in Lit. (C.H.13)

SUMMER SCHOOL

Faculty

SAMUEL K. MOSIMAN, A. M., Wittenberg, Ph. D., Halle.
President.

NOAH E. BYERS, B. S., Northwestern, A. M., Harvard.
Dean. Professor of Philosophy and Psychology.

EDMUND J. HIRSCHLER, A. B., Kansas, S. M., Chicago.
Registrar. Professor of Mathematics.

JOHN R. THIERSTEIN, A. B., Kansas, Ph. D., Bern.
Professor of German.

HARRY G. GOOD ,A. B., Indiana, Ph. D., Pennsylvania.
Professor of Education.

GUSTAV A. LEHMANN, A. B., Earlham, New York.
Instructor in Public School Music.

BOYD D. SMUCKER, O. M., King's School of Oratory.
Instructor in Oratory.

BEULAH S. ROBERTS, A. B., Kansas, Columbia.
Instructor in English.

BERTHA MASON, Ohio University.
Critic Teacher, Fourth and Fifth Grades.

FLOSSIE CAMPBELL, Miami, Bluffton.
Critic Teacher, First and Second Grades.
Instructor in Primary Methods.

Time

The Summer School of Bluffton College opens June 3 and continues during two terms of six weeks each, closing August 23. Monday of the first week will be devoted to the opening exercises and the registration of students. Instruction will begin on the following day.

Purpose

The Summer School is designed to meet the needs of the following classes of persons: (a) Teachers and those preparing to teach in the public elementary and secondary schools; (b) College students desiring credits counted toward the A. B. degree; (c) College preparatory and high school students desiring courses required for admission to college or for high school graduation.

Normal Courses

The training for teachers includes the subjects taught in the public, common and high schools and such professional courses that will in a practical way help the teacher to do his school room work more successfully. Opportunity will be given for observation and practice teaching under normal school room conditions.

College Courses

Such a variety of college courses is offered that any student can find work that will give credit on either the prescribed or elective requirements for the A. B. degree. Five hour courses for six weeks will give one and one-half and the double courses three semester credits. Bluffton College credits will be accepted in full, without examination by the leading colleges and universities. By taking several summers' work, a good student can complete the full college course in three years.

Preparatory Courses

High school and Academy students will be able to get courses to remove conditions or to shorten the time required to complete their work. Other courses than those offered may be given if called for by at least five students.

Faculty

The teaching staff is composed of persons thoroughly trained in their special subjects and in the theory and practice of teaching and have had wide experience both in public school work and in the training of teachers.

Lectures and Entertainments

Special lectures of interest to teachers will be given each week by leading educators for the purpose of giving practical help and professional enthusiasm.

Good talent is also being secured for musical and elocutionary entertainments.

Training School

Five grades of the Bluffton Schools will be used during the summer for observation and practice. The Critic teachers have been trained in standard normal schools and have had successful experience for a number of years. The instructors in Management and Methods will co-operate to make this a real model school for illustrating the best methods in the various grades.

Other Courses

Courses not listed in this bulletin may be offered if a sufficient number apply. For information address N. E. Byers, Dean, Bluffton, Ohio.

Expenses

A matriculation fee of $1.00 is charged each student entering the college for the first time. This fee is payable only once. Tuition is $10.00 per term of six weeks payable in advance. Rooms can be had in the Halls for $1.00, and board at Ropp Hall for men and women for $3.00 per week.

THE CONSERVATORY OF MUSIC

THE FACULTY

SAMUEL K. MOSIMAN .... President

GUSTAV ADOLF LEHMANN .... Dean

HAROLD B. ADAMS .... Organ and Pianoforte

MARK EVANS .... Singing

SIDNEY HAUENSTEIN .... Band and Orchestra

LEOLA PEARL BOGART .... Pianoforte

GAIL WATSON .... Violin

JULIA ACKERMANN ADAMS .... Theory

GUSTAV ADOLF LEHMANN .... Singing

MARTIN W. BAUMGARTNER .... Clarinet

BOYD D. SMUCKER .... Vocal Expression

ALICE MUELLER .... French

JOHN R. THIERSTEIN .... German

NOAH E. BYERS .... Psychology and Esthetics

HARRY G. GOOD .... Education

GENERAL STATEMENT

The Conservatory is a dictinct department of Bluffton College and thus subject to the general regulations of the College, but is under the immediate management of the Dean and the Conservatory Faculty.

It aims not only to teach the art of music in the noblest, fullest and highest sense, but also to encourage the development and the refinement of the minds, characters and tastes of its students under the influence of a Christian college. The Conservatory attempts for its students superior proficiency by a definite plan of study, not only for those wishing to devote themselves to music as teachers or artists, but also for amateurs whose chief aim is to acquire a correct knowledge of music. Thoroness is the motto of the Conservatory. The price for tuition has been made as low as possible consistent with its high aims. Conscientious teaching by broad-minded men and women of culture is the pride of the Conservatory.

One of the aims of the Conservatory is to foster in students of the College and Seminary a desire to know something of the history, esthetics and theory of the musical art.

PLAN OF EDUCATION

Students of the Conservatory are classified as Collegiate, Academic and Preparatory. Students, who satisfy the entrance requirements to the College of Liberal Arts and pursut one or more Conservatory Courses in Practic or Theoretic Music have Collegiate ranking. Students who pursue one or more Conservatory and one or more academic courses have academic ranking. Students, with academic or high school diploma, and who pursue only Conservatory courses have Preparatory ranking. Instruction in instrumental and vocal music is based largely on the private lesson system. Classes of a few may be arranged in extraordinary cases, but the most satisfactory results are obtained by careful attention to individual needs. Each student has his own mental, physical and artistic capacities, and personal attention alone can properly develop the fullest capabilities of the student.

The regular classes include the desirable elements of a

complete musical education. The musician should be more than a mere performer. True musicianship means a clear conception of the material of music, a firm grasp of fundamental artistic principles, and well defined and discriminating taste. All students are urged to take full courses, thus getting the benefit of the most favorable conditions in tuition and instruction.

Both Practic and Theoretic courses are included in the outline of courses and both demand a certain degree of advancement in general education.

COURSES

The following courses are offered:

I. Course in Practic Music, leading to the degree of Graduate in Music in case of Collegiate ranking, and to a Diploma of Musical Proficiency in case of Academy ranking.

II. Literary—Music Course, leading to degree of Bachelor of Arts.

III. Course in Public School Music, leading to the degree of Graduate in Public School Music.

I. COURSE IN PRACTIC MUSIC

By "Practic Music" is meant the practical study of pianoforte, organ, violin, cello or wind instrument playing, and singing, in private individual lessons. It also includes certain theoretical subjects scheduled below, which are given in classes. Completion of the courses is designed to equip students for professional work.

Students who are eligible to matriculate in the College of Liberal Arts will be given the College Diploma with the degree of Graduate in Music upon the satisfactory completion of the Course. Opportunity is given to make up reasonable deficiencies in College entrance requirements without extra expense. After payment of the matriculation fee students are permitted to pursue each year one College subject during the Music course without extra fee. Students registering for such subjects, however, are not permitted to drop their work except at the end of a semester, or if granted permission by the Dean of the Conservatory and the Dean of the College.

Students completing Course I as outlined below and furnishing credits for two years of academy or high school work will be given the Diploma of Musical Proficiency.

Students not desiring or unable to complete the studies necessary for matriculation in the College of Liberal Arts, may confine their work to the purely musical studies scheduled below, and upon satisfactory completion of the same are granted the Certificate of Musical Proficiency. Such students may carry one Academic study throughout the course without extra expense.

FIRST YEAR

College Choral Society, required of students in Singing.

College or Preparatory Study.

Ear Training and Dictation 9-10.

Ensemble Class Work, required of all students in their respective departments.

Harmony 13-14.

History of Music 17-18.

Orchestra and Band.

Practice Music, at least two half-hour periods per week.

Recitals.

Solfeggio 23-24, required of all students unless excused upon Dean's examination.

SECOND YEAR

Appreciation of Music 1-2.

Art of Accompanying. Chorus and Choir Training 5.

College Choral Society, required of students in Singing.

Counterpoint. Composition 7-8.

Form and Analysis 11-12.

Harmony 15-16.

History of Music 19-20.

Orchestra and Band.

Practic Music, at least two half-hour periods per week.

Recitals.

For detailed description of studies in Course I see later page.

Candidates for diploma in Course I must, in addition to completing the course outlined, satisfactorily meet the following requirements:

Piano and Organ Students—

(a) Must attend the weekly rehearsals of the College Choral Society unless excused by the Dean.

(b)   Perform satisfactorily a program conforming in general to the following outline:

(c)   Bach Prelude and Fugue; Beethoven Sonata; group of compositions from Mendelssohn, Schumann, Chopin, Liszt, MacDowell or other Masters.

Violin Students—

(a)   Must be in regular attendance of rehearsals of College Orchestra for at least two years.

(b)   Must play the piano fairly well.

(c)   Perform satisfactorily a program similar in general to the following outline: Bach Sonata; concerto with orchestral accompaniment.

Students in Singing—

(a)   Strictly regular attendance at weekly rehearsals of the College Choral Society.

(b)   College or Academy studies in the Freshman and Sophomore years must be German and French, one or the other each year, as the program of the individual student permits.

(c)   Must be able to play accompaniments well.

(d)   Must read vocal music at sight.

(e)   Perform satisfactorily a program similar, in general, to the following:

An operatic aria; an aria from Mendelssohn, Handel or Haydn; an aria from a modern oratorio; a group of songs from Schumann, Shubert, Franz or the like.

II.   LITERARY MUSIC COURSE

In harmony with the increasing demand for a collegiate training with Music as a Major, the College offers this course which leads to graduation with the degree of Bachelor of Arts upon completion of the following schedule of studies:

Bible .... 4 hours
Biology or Chemistry .... 8 hours
Electives .... 21 hours
English Literature and Composition .... 16 hours
German, French, Latin or Greek .... 24 hours
History and Economics .... 9 hours
Mathematics or Physics .... 3 hours
Music .... 24 hours

Philosophy .... 9 hours
Vocal Expression .... 2 hours
                                          —
                                        120

To enter this course students must meet the requirements of admission to the College of Liberal Arts.

Outline of Music Subjects Required in Literary-Music Course.

1. Practic Courses—The student may major in piano, organ or violin playing, or singing, and will be graduated upon the completion of any one of the following outlines in connection with the other collegiate work:

(a) Pianoforte and Organ—Completion of Grade III.
Piano Ensemble.
College Choral Society.

(b) Violin—Completion of Grade III.
Orchestra.
College Choral Society.

(c) Singing—Completion of Grade III.
Ear Training and Sight Reading.
College Choral Society.

2. Theoretic Courses.

FRESHMAN YEAR

Harmony 13-14.
History of Music 17-18.

SOPHOMORE YEAR

Harmony 15-16.

JUNIOR YEAR

History of Music 19-20.
Form and Analysis 11-12.

SENIOR YEAR

Counterpoint. Composition 7-8.
Appreciation of Music 1-2.

III. PUBLIC SCHOOL MUSIC COURSE
FIRST YEAR

First Semester	Hrs.	Second Semester	Hrs.
Voice	1	Voice	2
Piano	1	Piano	1
Solfeggio 23	1	Solfeggio 24	1
Harmony 13	2	Harmony 14	2
History of Music 17	2	History of Music 18	2
Psychology	3	Public and H. S. Methods	2
General Methods	5	School Management	2
		Principles of Education	3

SECOND YEAR

	Hrs.		Hrs.
		Voice	1
Voice	1	Piano	2
Piano	2	Harmony 16	2
Harmony 15	2	History of Music 20	2
History of Music 19	2	Composition and Counter-	
Composition and Counter-		point 8	1
point 7	1	Form and Analysis 12	1
Form and Analysis 11	1	Ear Training 10	1
Ear Training 9	1	Chorus and Conducting 5	2
Observation	2	School Administration	2
Appreciation 1	1	Practice Teaching	2
		Appreciation	1

DESCRIPTION OF THEORETIC COURSES

1-2. Appreciation of Music. One Hour, Two Semesters.
A study of the style and works of the important composers. Explanation of principles underlying all forms of musical composition. National characteristics. The nature and scope of music's expressive power.

Mrs. Adams.

3. Art of Accompanying. One Hour, First Semester.
Informal lectures and practical drill. Class lessons.

Mrs. Adams.

4. Psychology. Three Hours, First Semester.
Careful review of the beginnings and development of the

various physical and mental activities of the child.

                                        Professor Byers.

5. Chorus and Choir Training.   Two Hours, Second Semester.
Talks on conducting and the use of the baton. Technique
of beating time. Seating of chorus. Practice in chorus conducting by advanced students. Class lessons.

                                        Mr. Lehmann.

6. Church Music.   Three Hours, First Semester.
A thorough study of hymns and general church music.
Complete discussion of all phases of church music problems.

                                        Mr. Lehmann.

7-8. Counterpoint. Composition.   One Hour, Two Semesters.
Counterpoint in two, three, four and more parts.   Composition for voices and instruments.

                                        Mrs. Adams.

9-10. Ear Training and Dictation.   One Hour, Two Semesters.
Dictation of melodies, rhythms in key. Students taught
to recognize by ear and express in writing.

                                        Mr. Lehmann.

11-12. Form and Analysis.   One Hour, Two Semesters.
Typical forms of modern music. Analysis of chords and
of non-harmonic tones to be found in modern and classic
music.

                                        Mrs. Adams.

13-14. Harmony—Introductory.   Two Hours, Two Semesters.
Keys, Scales, Signatures, Intervals, Triads, Inversions,
Chord Connection, Cadences, Chords of the Seventh, Fig-
ured Chorales.

                                        Mrs. Adams.

15-16. Harmony—Advanced.   Two Hours, Two Semesters.
Modulation altered chords, suspensions and other non-
harmonic tones, Florid melody and accompaniment. Melody
writing.

                                        Mrs. Adams.

17-18. History of Music.   Two Hours, Two Semesters.
A general survey of musical history.

                                        Mrs. Adams.

19-20. History of Music.　　　　**Two Hours, Two Semesters.**
Modern Music. Critics and Criticism.

Mrs. Adams.

21. Normal Piano Methods.　　　**One Hour, Second Semester.**
Ear Training, Rhythm and Time Values. Notation, Sight-reading. Scale-building. Phrasing. Use of the Pedal. Teaching Materials. Questions and Answers. Practical Teaching. Class Lessons.

Professor Adams.

22. Public and High School Methods.

Two Hours, Second Semester.

Primary Grades—Recreation and rote songs. Monotones.
Intermediate Grades—Melody and Rhythm problems. Proportioning of exercises and songs. Chromatics and minors.
Grammar Grades—Part Songs. Modulations. Bass Staff.
High School—Codas and Choruses. How to teach high schools where music has never been taught. How to teach individual pupils who have had no previous training in music.

Mr. Lehmann.

23-24. Solfeggio.　　　　One Hour, **Two Semesters.**
Thorough drill in scale and interval singing. Class divided into two groups. Students of the beginners' section passed into the advanced section at the discretion of the instructor.

Mr. Lehmann.

25-26. Vocal Expression.　　　**Two Hours, Two Semesters.**
Exercises for good pronunciation. Modulation and tone quality, together with posture and gesture work.

Mr. Smucker.

College credit will be given for the following:
Appreciation of Music 1-2.
Child Study and Elementary Psychology 4.
Chorus and Choir Training 5.
Church Music 6.
Counterpoint. Composition 7-8.
Form and Analysis 11-12.
Harmony 13-16 inclusive.

History of Music 17-20 inclusive.
Vocal Expression 25-26.
Public and High School Methods 22.

Practic Courses

It is impossible to give a definite outline of the courses of study followed in the various courses of practic music because they vary more or less for each student.   Our plan is to adapt instruction to individual needs of the student.

The following lists of studies for piano, violin, organ and voice indicate the standard of technical difficulty in the various grades.

Each course in practic music is divided into three grades. All collegiate, academic and preparatory students are graded in practic music according to the degree of advancement in their respective course.

OUTLINE OF COURSES

1. Piano Playing.

Grade I.   Principles of tone production.   Study of five finger Exercises, Chords, Scales, Notations and Rhythm. Studies and Sonatinas selected from Czerny, Loeschorn, Gurlitt, Lichner, Bertini, Clementi; also easy compositions by classical and modern composers.

Grade II.   Continued study of Technique in every form. Short Preludes and Fugues and Inventions by Bach. Studies, Sonatas and Pieces selected from Czerny, Heller, Jensen, Cramer, Schubert, Beethoven, Haydn, Mozart, Mendelssohn; also additional compositions by modern composers.

Grade III. Difficult Studies, Preludes and Fugues,— Suites, Sonatas, Concertos and Pieces by Bach, Mozart, Beethoven, Grieg, Henselt, Liszt, Mendelssohn, Schumann, Rubinstein, Saint Saens, Chopin; also other classical and modern compositions.

Accompanying and Ensemble Course

A pianist's education is never complete without skill and experience in the subtle art of accompanying.   The small number of successful accompanists is due, not to the scarcity of good pianists, but to their deplorable lack of training and experience in ensemble playing.   This course is designed to meet the great demand for ensemble artists by developing in the pianist the ability to read at sight, a keen sense of tone values, an acute feeling of rhythm, development of the imagination, and a systematic disposition which puts the pianist "en rapport" with the composer and soloist.

2. **Violin Playing.**

Grade I.

Violin Methods of Polonaski, Schaedrick, de Beriot.

Etudes of Alard, Kayser, David.

School of Bowing Technique of O. Sevcik.

Solos of Dancla, Bohm, Sitt and Seitz.

Major and Minor Scales, Chords and Arpeggios.

Grade II. Etudes of Blumenstengel, Maza, Dout and Kreutzer.

Preparatory Technique of O. Sevcik.

Concertos of de Beriot, Viotti and Kreutzer.

Solos—Russian Arias of David, "Legende" of Wieniawski, "Eleggie of Ernst," "Mozurka" of Mylanaiski, "Ballade et Polonaise" Vieuxtemps.

Grade III. Etudes of Fivrillo, Rode, Dout.

Technical Studies of Sevcik and Siebert.

Concertos of Rode, Spohr, Mendelssohn, Mozart, Wieniawski.

Sonatas—Handel, A Major; Tartim, G Minor.

Solos—"Mazurka" of Musin, "Zigeunerweisen" of Sarasate.

"Romance" of Beethoven, "Souvenir de Moscou" of Wieniawski.

Orchestra—Registered members of College Orchestra will be given practic music credit in the Conservatory.

3. **Organ Playing.**

To secure the best results from organ study, the pupil should be thoroughly grounded in piano technique and in the studies making for a broad Musicianship—Harmony, History, etc. And it is expected that the student continue these studies during the full organ course. A bare outline of three grades' work is here given.

Nilson Pedal Studies.

Master Studies for the Organ, by William Carl.

Organ Compositions—Bach. Together with selections from German, French, English, Italian and American composers.

Choir and Congregational Accompanying.

4. Singing.

Cultivation of the voice in singing is now regarded as an important branch of education, yet probably no branch in culture has been so much neglected as that which relates to the development of the voice. In the study of the voice much care is taken toward forming a good technical foundation which is just as important in a singer's career as in that of a pianist.

In forming this basis particular attention is given to the following essential points: (1) A correct intonation; (2) a good and easy execution; (3) a clear and distinct pronunciation; (4) an intelligent expression which embraces all the lights and shades, colorings and artistic rendition of a piece of music. To sing well requires a thorough knowledge of the voice and how to use it. This means a knowledge of the proper control of breathing. Much care is taken in developing interpretative ability and in trying to cultivate in the student an artistic taste and an appreciation of the best works of art.

Grade I. Principles of breathing as applied to tone production. Voice Placing, Vocalization, Enunciation, Exercises from Behnke and Abt and Study of Ballads.

Grade II. Principles of breathing, etc., continued throughout the course according to the requirements of each individual pupil. Solfeggio by the best writers, continued Vocalization and Study of the more difficult Ballads and Classic Songs.

Grade III. Advanced Vocalization, Difficult Solfeggio. Study of the best songs from Schubert, Franz, Brahms, Grieg, Wolf, McDowell and others.

Such exercises will be used as requirements may demand. Continued use of songs from the best of the modern writers and from the old masters.

Selections from the great Oratorios and Operas.

Ensemble Classes   One Hour, Two Semesters.

To develop the ability to sing accurately and independently in ensemble should be a part of the training of every student and the conservatory maintains these classes throughout the course. Duets, trios and quartets are studied in class and prepared for public recital.

Mr. Lehmann.

Choral Singing.

Singing in a large choral society offers the best preparation for church choir singing and is an excellent means for the development of ability in sight reading and rhythm discernment.

The College Choral Society appears several times each year and the best compositions of modern and classic writers are studied. Regular Conservatory students are expected to be members, but membership is open to students in all departments and to the singers in the town and community. Student members are given practic music credit on recommendation of the director.

Vesper Choir.

The Vesper Choir is a body of twenty-five singers, selected from the College and community. Vacancies are filled by the officers and the choir, and Conservatory students with sufficient singing ability are eligible for membership. Conservatory faculty members are in charge of this organization. Student members are given practic music credit on recommendation of the director.

TUITION FEES

All private lessons thirty minutes.
All class lessons one hour.

Organ and Piano

Professor Adams.

One-half semester, one lesson per week............$10.00
One semester, one lesson per week.................. 18.00
One-half semester, two lessons per week............ 18.00
One semester, two lessons per week................. 34.00

Miss Bogart.

One-half semester, one lesson per week.............$ 8.00
One semester, one lesson per week................. 14.00
One-half semester, two lessons per week........... 14.00
One semester, two lessons per week............... 26.00

Piano Accompanying and Ensemble

Professor Adams.

Mrs. Adams.

Miss Bogart.

One-half semester, one lesson per week............$ 3.00
One semester, one lesson per week................. 5.00

Violin

Miss Watson.

One-half semester, one lesson per week.............$10.00
One semester, one lesson per week................. 18.00
One-half semester, two lessons per week........... 18.00
One semester, two lessons per week............... 34.00

Orchestra and Band Instruments

Mr. Hauenstein.

One-half semester, one lesson per week............$ 8.00
One semester, one lesson per week................. 14.00
One-half semester, two lessons per week........... 14.00
One semester, two lessons per week............... 26.00

Ensemble Classes

Orchestra .... Entrance and semester fees
Band .... Entrance fees

Singing

Mr. Evans.

Mr. Lehmann.

One-half semseter, one lesson per week............$10.00
One semester, one lesson per week................. 18.00
One-half semester, two lessons per week........... 18.00
One semester, two lessons per week............... 34.00

Ensemble for Singers

Mr. Lehmann.

One-half semester, one hour per week.............$ 3.00
One semester, one hour per week.................$ 5.00

Choral Singing

College Choral Society ¦...... Entrance and semester fees
Vesper Choir .... Fee on examination

Vocal Expression

r. Smucker.

One semester, two hours per week....................$ 5.00
One semester, one hour per week, private.......... 15.00

Theory Courses

Mrs. Adams.

One semester, one hour per week....................$ 5.00
One semester, two hours per week.................. 9.00
One semester, three hours per week....   ......12..00

The College year is divided into semesters, and students will pay at least one-half semester in advance. Preparatory or resident students may enter practic courses at any time but are required to pay in advance to the end of the semester in which they register. Students are required to present coupon books to instructor before each lesson.

Students registered in Literary-Music Course receive a rebate of $25.00 on the regular College Tuition.

Rent of Piano for Practice

One-half Semester:

One hour each day ....$ 3.00
Two hours each day 5.00
Three hours each day 7.00
Four hours each day 8.50
Five hours each day 10.00

One Semester:

One hour each day ....$ 5.00
Two hours each day 9.00
Three hours each day 13.00
Four hours each day 16.00
Five hours each day 19.00
Vocal Students .... One-half of above rates

Rent of Organ for Practice

Twenty-five cents per hour.

Matriculation Fee

A matriculation fee of one dollar is charged each student. This is paid but once.

Diploma Fee

The diploma fee is five dollars.

College Music Course Ticket, two dollars.

Free Courses—Solfeggio and Ear-training classes, faculty concerts, numerous recitals and lectures in the College are open to the Conservatory and College students.

Refunds

Private lessons falling upon legal holidays are made up at the convenience of the instructors. No deductions are allowed for occasional absences due to illness or other causes. If due notice be given of the necessity for extended absence on account of sickness, private lessons missed after such due notice will be transferred to a later semester. Absences without such proper notice cannot receive such consideration.

One-half the fee for class lessons or practice is refunded to a student who withdraws before the ninth week of a semester, provided he secures from the Dean a statement of honorable standing, and from a physician a certificate that his health does not permit him to remain in attendance.

GENERAL INFORMATION

Chapel attendance is required of all regular Conservatory students unless excused by the Dean of the College or the Dean of Women.

All Conservatory students are subject to the general College discipline.

Class grades of Conservatory students are placed with Registrar on the basis adopted by the College.

Students or those contemplating study, are invited to consult freely with the Dean concerning their studies, their plans for work and whatever may require their attention.

Special arrangements will be made for students residing out of town and wishing to come to Bluffton only on lesson days.

Students pursuing regular courses in the Conservatory are required to attend all recitals and concerts.

Students are urged to consult their teacher before appearing in public performances.

Students may have the use of the Gymnasium by paying the fee of $1.50 per semester.

The Conservatory offers several courses in Piano, Singing and Theory during the Summer.

Parents sometimes fail to realize that early study develops masters. The Conservatory encourages local people to start their children in the Preparatory department.

For special information regarding the Conservatory, address THE, DEAN, Bluffton College Conservatory of Music Bluffton, Ohio.

MENNONITE SEMINARY

FACULTY

REV. SAMUEL K. MOSIMAN, President,
Professor of Old Testament Language and Literature.

REV. JACOB H. LANGENWALTER, Dean,
Professor of Systematic and Practical Theology.

REV. JASPER A. HUFFMAN,
Professor of New Testament Language and Literature.

REV. PAUL E. WHITMER,
Professor of Church History.

NOAH E. BYERS,
Professor of Philosophy and Religious Education.

C. HENRY SMITH,
Professor of History and Social Sciences.

GUSTAV ADOLF LEHMANN,
Instructor in Church Music.

BOYD D. SMUCKER,
Instructor in Public Speaking.

REV. W. H. LAHR,
Instructor in Hebrew.

SPECIAL LECTURER

EDWIN McNEIL POTEAT,
Lecturer on Bible Teaching.

MENNONITE SEMINARY

PURPOSE

Mennonite Seminary was founded primarily to serve the special needs of the Mennonite churches of America but is open to students of any denomination. This seminary is an answer to the oft-repeated request that an opportunity should be offered to the young men and the young women of the various branches of the Mennonite church, who are willing to enter the service of the kingdom of God, to fit themselves more thoroughly for this kind of work.

The opportunities of this age are so large that they become an irresistable call to the man or woman with a vision. Such men and women need and desire an adequate preparation. To offer them such training as will enable them to work effectively in the kingdom of God and at the same time serve through the activities of their own church, is the aim of the Mennonite Seminary.

MISSIONS

The Seminary is developing a special department for candidates for the Foreign Mission fields, and every effort will be made to meet the needs of such candidates by arranging work for them with a view to their previous preparation, the time at their disposal for further preparation and the particular field which they expect to enter.

There are a number of courses in the Seminary curriculum which are as valuable for the workers in the Foreign field as for those in the Home fields, and which will be taught with the needs and the interests of the former in mind. These facts afford an increase of opportunities for candidates for the Foreign Mission fields beyond those suggested by the courses especially designed for their benefit. More specific information will gladly be given on application.

GRADUATION

Students desiring to graduate from the regular course in the Seminary must present evidence of having done the equivalent of work required for graduation from a recognized college; must be members in good standing of some Christian church; must, during their connection with the Seminary, give evidence of a Christian character and of ability to enter the field of some Christian activity and do its work successfully; they must complete with credit at least 90 semester hours, not more than 20 of which may have been counted toward entrance requirements. The degree of Bachelor of Divinity (B. D.) is conferred upon those who complete the course with high standing.

Candidates for the A. M. degree may select certain courses, approved by the College Committee on Graduate Studies, from the curriculum of the Seminary. The conditions, which apply when work is selected from the Seminary courses, are the same as those prescribed for candidates for the A. M. degree in any department of the College of Liberal Arts.

Courses selected from the Seminary curriculum may be counted toward both the A. M. and B. D. degrees, but the B. D. degree will not be granted until the completion of 90 hours of high grade work, none of which has been counted toward the A. B. degree.

DEPARTMENTS OF INSTRUCTION

The work of the Seminary is listed under nine departments of instruction arranged as follows:

Old Testament .... O. T.

New Testament .... N. T.

Philosophy of Religion and Religious Education..P. R.

Systematic Theology .... S. Th.

Sociology .... H.

Church History and Doctrines .... C. H.

Homiletics and Practical Theology .... P. Th.

Comparative Religions and Christian Missions.... Mi.

Public Speaking .... E.

Church Music .... Mu.

All courses in the English department are listed....B.

COURSES OF INSTRUCTION

The courses outlined in this catalog show the type of work that Mennonite Seminary offers.

The number of hours credit is indicated in each course. An hour is one class period a week for one semester.

OLD TESTAMENT
Professor Whitmer

1-2. Old Testament History and Religion.
Three Hours, Two Semesters.

This course embraces a study of the historical movements, literary products and religious ideas from the establishment of the kingdom under Saul to the restoration of the kingdom under Ezra-Nehemiah. The activities and writings of the prophets will receive chief emphasis.

Professor Huffman

3-4. Old Testament Theology.   **Two Hours, Two Semesters.**

The Revelation of God as He progressively revealed Himself and His will in Old Testament times will be carefully studied. Special attention will be given to the Christology of the Old Testament, noting the types, figures and prophecies, pointing to His advent and mission. The Bible will be the principal text. Huffman's Old Testament Messages of the Christ will also be used. Not given 1918-19.

President Mosiman

5-6. Hebrew Language.   **Four Hours, Two Semesters.**

The class is expected to master the general principles of orthography, the inflection of the verb and noun as well as the reading of easy prose and a few Psalms. A Hebrew Bible, a Lexicon and Harper's Manual and Elements are text-books used.

7. Hebrew Exegesis.   **Three Hours, First Semester.**

The course will include the Exegesis of special passages in Exodus and the Exegesis of special Psalms. Not given 1918-19.

. Hebrew Prose. Three Hours, Second Semester.
The object of the course will be to give an opportunity
for rapid reading and the acquiring of a vocabulary. Not
given 1918-19.

. The Psalms. Three Hours, First Semester.
A study of the origin, structure, interpretation and religious teaching of the Psalms. Not given 1918-19.

0. Hebrew. Three Hours, Second Semester.
A study of Isaiah, chapters 1-39. Not given 1918-19.

NEW TESTAMENT
Professor Whitmer

-2. Apostolic Christianity. Three Hours, Two Semesters.
The first semester will be devoted to a critico-historical
study of Galatians, parts of First and Second Corinthians
and Romans with a cursory survey of Paul's minor epistles.
The course aims to give a thorough understanding of the
Pauline system. In the second semester a similar study will
be made of Hebrews and the Epistles of John, James and
Peter. Not given 1918-19.

Professor Huffman

-4. New Testament Theology. Two Hours, Two Semesters.
This work will constitute an investigation of the doctrines
of the New Testament, as they relate to individuals and the
church. The Bible will be the principal text-book, and information will be gathered from every available source. Not
given 1918-19.

-6. Greek Exegesis. Three Hours, Two Semesters.
Reading and exegetical work will be confined principally
to selections from the Gospels and Johannean epistles. Special attention will be given to grammatical construction, developing the student for the more difficult work of the following years. Westcott and Hort's Greek Text will be used
throughout.

-8. Greek Exegesis. Three Hours, Two Semesters.
The Harmony of the Gospels will be studied in the Greek,
also several epistles. Robinson's Greek Harmony will be
used for work in harmony.

9-10. Greek Exegesis.   Three Hours, Two Semesters.

The exegetical work of the Senior year will be largely confined to the Pauline Epistles. Boice's Notes will be employed as special helps. Not given 1918-19.

PHILOSOPHY OF RELIGION AND RELIGIOUS EDUCATION
Professor Byers

3. Child Psychology.   Three Hours, First Semester.

The characteristics of the different periods of childhood and youth are studied. Special attention is given to the study of the instincts and the means by which they may be developed into useful reaction or serve as a starting point for mental development.

4. Educational Psychology.   Three Hours, Second Semester.

A study of the psychological basis of the educative process. Special attention will be given to such topics as interest, attention, apperception, memory, habits and discipline, considered with special reference to the work of the teacher. Text-book and supplementary reading.

8. Ethics.   Three Hours, Second Semester.

A critical and comparative study is made of the leading schools of ethics, followed by the formulation of a theory of the moral life and its application to modern, social and economic problems. Wide reading of texts and the works of leading ethical philosophers, lectures and theses.

17. Modern Idealism.   Three Hours, First Semseter.

An advanced course in metaphysics, based upon Royce's "The World and the Individual." This is a study of the first principles of philosophy as a basis for a philosophy of religion. Not given 1918-19.

18. Contemporary Philosophy.   Three Hours, Second Semester.

A critical study of recent philosophical movements. Special attention will be given to the Philosophies of James, Eucken and Bergson, noting in particular their influence on the religious thought of today. Not given 1918-19.

Psychology of Religion. **Two Hours, First Semester.**

A psychological study of religious experience. Special attention is given to the study of the adolescent period and the psychology of conversion. A critical study is made of the literature of the subject.

Philosophy of Religion. **Two Hours, Second Semester.**

This is a study of the fundamental principles of religion as related to philosophy and science and seeks to aid the student in acquiring freedom in critical thinking, and in gaining a unified view of the world in which religious truth and life find their proper place.

Religious Education. **Two Hours, First Semester.**

This course should be preceded by courses 3 and 4. The pedagogy of religious teaching and training and the teaching work of the church. A study will be made of the various methods by which Bible teaching in the church is correlated with the work of the public schools. Not given 1918-19.

The Sunday School. **Two Hours, Second Semester.**

This course follows 21 and aims to apply the principles of Religious Education to the work of the Sunday School. Special attention is given to aim, organization, courses of study and methods of teaching. Opportunity will be given for observation and practice teaching under the supervision of the instructor in charge. Not given 1918-19.

SYSTEMATIC THEOLOGY
Professor Langenwalter

Introduction to Theology. **Three Hours, First Semester.**

This course comprises a study of religion as a natural phenomenon, its development into the Christian religion; the need of man for religion under his various conditions; the nature of religious knowledge, faith and doubt; the Christian world-view as compared with other world-views, the justification of the Christian religion, based on experience, history and interpretation. Not given 1918-19.

Distinctive Truths of Christianity.

Three Hours, Second Semester.

This course deals with the Christian idea of religion,

God and the Trinity; the world in its relation to God and
His purposes; the idea of man, his needs and his place in
the universe; the place of Jesus, considered from the viewpoint of His nature, His historic career and His abiding
significance; the importance of the Spirit of God for the
Christian life; the questions of sin, death, immortality and
kindred problems.   These topics will be approached both
from the Biblical and the philosophical viewpoint. Not giv-
en 1918-19.

3-4. Christian Ethics.   Two Hours, Two Semesters.

This course will involve a study of the development of
ethical thought arising from the use of the Christian Scriptures; a comparison of the type of ethics evolved from the
Christian Scriptures with other types and a study of the
application of the principles of Christian ethics to the problems of modern society.

SOCIOLOGY
Professor Smith

19. The Principles of Sociology.   Three Hrs., First Semester.

A brief elementary course aiming to give a survey of the
entire field of the Science of Society.   The study includes
a brief examination of the nature of social order, social evolution, the factors of social progress, the structure of society.   A brief study will also be made of the most pressing
social problems before our country, such as crime, poverty,
effects of immigration, negro problem, and attention will
also be paid to recent social legislation.

17. Social Legislation.   Two Hours, First Semester.

A survey of recent legislation on social and economic
questions enacted and proposed in various states. Not giv-
en 1918-19.

18. Rural Sociology.   Two Hours, Second Semester.

A discussion of the social problems of the open country,
rural education, recreation, health, country church, and the
various institutions and movements which are connected
with a wholesome country life.

Socialism and Social Reform. Three Hrs., Second Semester.

This course covers the theory and history of early schemes for social reform from Plato to the present and includes a study of communism and anarchism. Present socialism in Europe and America will be studied both from the great writers on the subject as well as from contemporary and current literature. The work will be largely in the form of lectures with outside reading. Not given 1918-19.

CHURCH HISTORY AND DOCTRINES
Professor Whitmer
History of the Christian Church.

Three Hours, First Semester.

A survey of the history of the Christian church from its beginnings to the Reformation, emphasizing the Apostolic church, the spread of Christianity in the Graeco-Roman world, early heresies and schisms, ecumenical councils, the crusades, monasticism, scholasticism, the Christianization of the Germanic peoples, the decline of the papacy, the renaissance and the sects and movements preparatory to the Reformation.

History of the Christian Church.

Three Hours, Second Semester.

From the Reformation to the present time. The Reformation, the Counter-Reformation, the rise and the development of the Protestant denominations in Europe, England and America with a study of their beliefs, worship and organization.

American Christianity.   Two Hours, First Semester.

A brief history of the pre-Reformation Evangelical sects, and the relation of Church and State during the Colonial period, the great religious awakenings, the Revolutionary and Civil Wars in their effects upon the churches, and development of religious thought of more recent years. The American Church History Series furnish the basis for the class work.

The Mennonites.   Two Hours, Second Semester.

A brief survey of the early beginnings and later development of the various Christian bodies in the United States, and Anabaptists with which the Mennonite movement was closely related, and the development of the Mennonite Church to the present. Half of the course will be devoted to Europe and the other half to America. Special attention will be paid to the sociological as well as the historical phase of the subject. Largely lectures with assigned reading in library.

7. History of Christian Doctrine. **Two Hours, First Semester.**
The development of Christian doctrine from the apostolic age to the Reformation. The work will be grouped about the great leaders of the Christian church; the Apostolic Fathers, the Apologists, the Alexandrines, the Latin and Catholic churchmen and writers. Not given 1918-19.

8. History of Christian Doctrine. **Two Hours, Second Semester.**
From the Reformation to the present time. The doctrinal teachings of Luther, Melanchthon, Calvin, Zwingli, Menno Simons and others will be studied. The influence of these teachings will be traced in the development of the Church in Europe, England and America. The great Protestant creeds will be studied and compared. Not given in 1918-19.

11-12. The Bible in Poetry. Three Hours, Two Semesters.
The chief object of this course will be to trace and evaluate the Biblical and ethical ideas in several great literary masterpieces. The following selections are representative of the masterpieces to be studied: Dante's "Divine Comedy," Shakespeare's Tragedies, Milton's "Paradise Lost," Wordsworth's "Prelude," Goethe's "Faust," Tennyson's "In Memoriam" and Browning's "Saul" and "Rabbi Ben Ezra." Not given 1918-19.

13-14. The Bible in Modern Prose.
Three Hours, Two Semesters.
A closer acquaintance with the prose literature which deals with life problems and ideals is the chief aim of this year's work. The works studied will be selected from the following: Johnson's "Rasselas," Eliot's "Romola," De-Quincey's "Confessions," Reade's "Cloister and the Hearth," Carlyle's "Sartor Resartus," Newman's "Apologie pro Vita Sua," Thackeray's "Vanity Fair," Aronld's "Culture and An-

archy," Hugo's "Les Miserables" and Tolstoy's "Anna Karanina."

Open to Seniors and qualified Juniors.

HOMILETICS AND PRACTICAL THEOLOGY*
Professor Langenwalter

1. **Homiletics.** **Two Hours, First Semester.**
    The aim of this course is to outline the work of preach-
ing; to study the several types of sermons, supplementing
this study with preparation, delivery and discussion of each
type of sermon. Not given 1918-19.

2. **Homiletics.** **Two Hours, Second Semester.**
    The plan of work outlined in Course 1 will be continued
and, in addition, the biographies and productions of a number of great preachers will be studied. Not given 1918-19.

3. **Homiletics.** **Two Hours, First Semester.**
    The purpose of this course is to study the Bible from the
preacher's standpoint. The expository sermon will receive
special emphasis in view of the fact that this course is
meant to be of special benefit to the students preparing for
the mission field as well as those intending to enter the ministry.

4. **Homiletics.** **Two Hours, Second Semester.**
    A study of the practical questions which face the preach-
er in the selection of the themes on which he is to preach.
Special days, events and questions confronting the Christian
church today will be considered and sermons will be prepared, delivered and discussed so as to prepare the student
to meet these questions in the pastorate or on the mission
field.

5. **Introduction to the Study of Religion.**
    Two Hours, First Semester.
    The purpose of this course is to give the student a prelim-
inary survey of the possibilities of a course in a Seminary or
School of Religion.

7. **Social Gospel of Jesus.** **Two Hours, First Semester.**
    The development and modern status of problems con-
cerning the state, the family and society in general will be

viewed from the angle suggested by the teachings of Jesus. Emphasis will also be laid upon those portions of the Old Testament which Jesus evidently had in mind in connection with the up-building of His "kingdom."

8. **Rural Church Problems.** **Two Hours, Second Semester.**
A study of the problems confronting the churches in rural communities, villages and small towns. This phase of the church problems is of particular interest to the Mennonite churches of America at this time. This fact will receive special consideration in this course.

9-10. **Church Administration.** **Three Hours, Two Semesters.**
A study of the church, its place in the community, its functions, its obligations to those who need it. Various types of fields will be studied as to their opportunities and difficulties. Methods for conducting the work of the church as advantageously as possible will be examined and discussed. There will also be a careful study of the various auxiliary organizations of the church as to organization, relation to the church, efficiency, opportunity. Special attention will be paid to the problems of church unity and church polity. This course is required of Seniors.

COMPARATIVE RELIGIONS AND CHRISTIAN MISSIONS

1. **Comparative Religions.** **Two Hours, First Semester.**
A study of the various religions, which are active agents in modern society. Not given 1918-19.

2. **History of Christian Missions.** **Two Hrs., Second Semester.**
A historical survey of the missionary activities of the Christian church from their beginnings to the present time. Special emphasis will be laid upon the developments within the last few generations.

3. **Mission Fields.** **Two Hours, First Semester.**
A critical study of the opportunities for Christian missions; the particular fields to be selected and reasons for so doing; the equipment of those who are to enter these fields as societies, and more directly as missionaries with a view to civilizing, evangelizing and Christianizing the inhabitants of the fields in question.

4. Mennonite Mission Felds. **Two Hours, Second Semester.**

A study of the founding, growth and present status of the various Mennonite mission stations, both in the foreign and the home field. Any missionary enterprise of any branch of the Mennonites whatsoever, is to be included in this study. Some time will also be devoted to the work done by various Mennonite institutions, e. g., schools, philanthropic institutions, etc. Special emphasis will be laid upon the bearing which the work of these institutions may have upon the spirit and work of missions.

6. A Philosophy of Missions. **Two Hours, Second Semester.**

This course was developed in answer to the frequently presented question: "What type of thinking makes for a valid interest in Missions?" The work consists of assigned readings, reports and class discussions. Not given 1918-19.

PUBLIC SPEAKING

Mr. Smucker

1. Practical Elocution Course. **Two Hours, First Semester.**

The fundamentals of Public Speaking are emphasized in this course. Special attention is given to pronunciation, tone-placing, posture and gesture. Selections will be committed and recited before the class. "Fulton and Trueblood" will probably be used as a text.

2. Argumentation and Debate. **Two Hours, Second Semester.**

Gardiner's "The Making of Arguments" will probably be used as a text with practical work in the class room for delivery.

3-4. Bible and Hymn Reading. **Two Hours, Two Semesters.**

This course is especially designed to meet the needs of the Seminary students and will include interpretive Bible Reading, the classification of poems, sonnets, orations and the analysis of hymns.

Private work will be given in this department and other classes organized if a sufficient number apply.

CHURCH MUSIC
Mr. Lehmann

23-24. Solfeggio. One **Hour, Two Semesters.**
Thorough drill in scale and interval singing. Class divided into two groups. Students of Beginners' section passed into Advanced section at the discretion of the instructor.
Texts—Beginners: "Melodia"—Lewis and Cole.
Advanced: "Harmonia"—Lewis and Cole.

5. Church Music. Three **Hours, First Semester.**
The selection and study of hymns and hymn tunes. Instruction in congregational singing and the directing of congregational singing. Students are urged to enter the Solfeggio class before registering in this course.

6. Chorus and Choir Training. **Two Hours, Second Semester.**
Talks on conducting and the use of the baton. Technique of beating time. Seating of Chorus. Practice in conducting chorus by advanced students.

Other courses in the Conservatory are open to Theological students.

SEMINARY COURSES OF STUDY
First Semester 1918-19

Required	No. Hrs.

Junior Year

Two years of O. T. work will be required before graduation.

Three years of N. T. will be required before graduation, two of which must be N. T. Greek for the B. D. degree.

3, 7 or 21 Phil. of Rel. and Rel. Educ. will be required before the end of the Middle Year.

History of Christian Church 1 3

Homiletics 1 2

Middle Year

Introduction to Theology ..3

History of Christian Doctrine 7 2

(Required for the B. D. degree)

Senior Year

Church Administration ...3

Electives	Hrs.

Old Testament
O. T. History and Religion 1.3
O. T. Theol. 3 2
Hebrew Language 5 4
Hebrew Exegesis 7 3
The Psalms 9 3

New Testament
Apostolic Christianity 3
N. T. Theol. 3 2
Greek Exegesis 5 3
Greek Exegesis 7 3
Greek Exegesis 9 3

Phil. of Rel. and Rel. Educ.
Child Psychology 3 3
Modern Idealism 17 3
Psychol. of Rel. 7 2
Religious Education 21 2

Systematic Theology
Christian Ethics 3 2

Sociology
Social Legislation 17 2
Principles of Sociology 19   3

Church History
Amer. Christianity 3 2
History of the Chr. Doctrine 7
.....................2
The Bible in Literature 11...3

Hom. and Pract. Theology
Homiletics 3 2
Introd. to the Study of Rel. 5
.....................2
Social Gospel of Jesus 7 2

Comp. Rel. and Chr. Missions
Comparative Religions 1 2
Mission Fields 3 2

Public Speaking
Practical Elocution 1 2
Bible and Hymn Reading 3 ..2

Church Music
Solfeggio 23 1
Church Music 5........... 2

SEMINARY COURSES OF STUDY
Second Semester 1918-19

Required	No. Hrs.

Junior Year

Two years of O. T. work will be required before graduation.

Three years of N. T. work will be required before graduation, two of which must be N. T. Greek for the B. D. degree.

4, 6, 14 or 22 Phil. of Rel. and Rel. Educ. will be required before the end of the Middle Year.

History of the Christian Church 2 2

Homiletics 2 2

Middle Year

Distinctive Truths of Christianity 2 3

History of Christian Doctrine 8 2

(Required of candidates for the B. D. degree)

Senior Year

Church Administration 4..3

Electives	Hrs.

O. T. History and Religion 2 3
O. T. Theology 4 2
Hebrew Language 6 4
Hebrew Prose 8 3
Hebrew 10 3

New Testament
Apostolic Christianity 2 3
N. T. Theology 4 2
Greek Exegesis 6 3
Greek Exegesis 8 3
Greek Exegesis 10 3
Phil. of Rel. and Rel. Education
Educ. Psychology 4 3
Ethics 8 3
Contemporary Phil. 18 3
Phil. of Religion 14 2
Sunday School 22 2

Systematic Theology
Christian Ethics 4 2

Sociology
Rural Sociology 18 2
Socialism and Social Reform 20 3

Church History
The Mennonites 4 2
History of Church Doctr. 8..2
The Bible as Literature 12..3
Homiletics and Prac. Theol.
Homiletics 4 2
Rural Church Problems 8 ...2
Comp. Religions and Missions
History of Christian Missions 2 2
Mennonite Mission Fields 4 2
Phil. of Missions 6.. 2
Public Speaking
Argument and Debate 2 2
Bible and Hymn Reading 4..2
Church Music
Solfeggio 24 1
Chorus and Choir Training 6 3

SEMINARY SCHEDULE OF LECTURES AND RECITATIONS FOR

THE FIRST SEMESTER, 1918-19

Instructors	7:45	8:40	9:35	10:30	10:50	1:00	2:00	3:00
Langenwalter	Chr. Ethics (S. Th. 3) W. F.	Mod. Prob. O. T. (B. 13) W. F. Th. / Soc. Gosp. (P. Th. 7) W. F.	Homiletics (P. Th. 3) W. F. / Ch. Admin. (P. Th. 9) T. Th. S.	CHAPEL			Miss. Fields (Mi. 3) W. F.	
Huffman	Greek (A. L. 1) W. Th. F. S.	Pentateuch (B. 5) W. F. / Greek (N. T. 7) T. Th. S.	Syn. B. Study (B. 1) T. Th. S.		Greek (N. T. 5) T. Th. S.			
Whitmer		His. Chr. Ch. (C. H. 1) T. Th. S. / Amer. Chr. (C. H. 3) W. F.			N. T. (B. 11) W. F. / O. T. Hist. & Rel. (O. T. 1) T. Th. S. / Psy. of Rel. (P. R. 7) W. F.			Bible in Mod. Prose (C. H. 13) T. Th. S.
Byers	Child Psychology (P. 3) T. Th. S.		Sociology (H. 19) T. Th. S.					
Smith	Church Mu. T. Th. S.							
Lehmann								
Smucker	P. Speaking (E. 15) T. S.							

SEMINARY SCHEDULE OF LECTURES AND RECITATIONS FOR

THE SECOND SEMESTER, 1918-19

Instructors	7:45	8:40	9:35	10:30	10:50	1:00	2:00	3:00
Langenwalter	Chr. Ethics (S. Th. 4) W. F.	Mod. Prob. O. T. (B 14) T. Th. Rural Ch. Pr. (P. Th. 8) W. F.	Ch. Admin. (P. Th. 10) T. Th. S. Homiletics (P. Th. 4) W. F.				Hist. Chr. Missions (Mi. 2) W. F.	
Huffman	Greek (A. L. 2) T. W. Th. S.	Prophecy (B. 6) W. F. Greek (N. T. 8) T. Th. S.	Syn. B. Study (B. 2) T. Th. S.		Greek (N. T. 6) T. Th. S.			
Whitmer		His. Chr. Ch. (C. H. 2) T. Th. S. The Menn. (C. H. 4) W. F.			N.T. (B. 12) W. F. O. T. Hist. & Rel. (O. T. 2) T. Th. S.			Bible in Mod. Prose (C. H. 14) T. Th. S.
Byers	Educ. Psych. (P. 4) T. Th. S.				Phil. of Rel. (P. R. 14) W. F.		Ethics (P. R. 8) T. W. F.	
Smith			Rural Soc. (H. 18) T. Th. S.					
Lehmann	Chorus and Choir W. F.							
Smucker	Debating (E. 16) F. S.							

10:30 — CHAPEL

ENGLISH DEPARTMENT

In order to meet the needs of those who are not in position to enter the Graduate Course of the Seminary, an English Course has been arranged. Before completing this course every student will be required to have had, at least, an equivalent of ten semester hours of College English and six semester hours of College History.

The completion of this course entitles the student to a diploma of graduation. The conditions for graduation are: (a) membership in good standing in some Christian church; (b) a creditable completion of at least ninety semester hours of work, including all of the prescribed work, but not including the English and History referred to above; (c) evidence of fitness and ability to enter upon the duties of the Christian Ministry, the Foreign or Home Mission Field, the Deaconess Work, etc., honorably; (d) the payment of a Diploma Fee of three dollars, in accordance with the regulations of the Board of Directors.

Students of sufficient ability and training may, with the advice of the Faculty, choose courses offered in the Graduate Department of the Seminary.

COURSES OF INSTRUCTION
Professor Huffman

1-2. Synthetic Bible Study.　　　Three Hours, Two Semesters.

This course affords a study of the various books of the Bible in their relation to the Bible as a whole. Each book is examined as to authorship, date, contents, etc., and as to the particular contribution which it makes to God's revelation of Himself through His Word. The Bible is the principal text. Other suitable helps will be employed. This is a good foundation course for further Bible study.

3-4. Old Testament History.　　　Two Hours, Two Semesters.

This study covers the history of Israel from the call of Abraham to the rebuilding of the temple upon their return from captivity. The development of their religious and civil institutions will be carefully studied. Dr. William Smith's Old Testament History will be used. Not given 1918-19.

5. Pentateuch and Historical **Books.**

Two Hours, First Semester.

Special attention will be given to the Pentateuch, and as much time as possible will be devoted to the other Historical Books.   Recent archaeological investigations will be studied in their relation to the historical and scientific accuracy of the Bible.

6. Prophecy, Psalms and **Wisdom Literature.**

Two Hours, Second Semester.

Prophecy will be studied especially in relation to its Messianic aspect.   The student will be familiarized with Hebrew poetry.   The Wisdom Literature will be studied with special attention devoted to the Book of Job.

7. Harmony of the Gospels (English.)

Two Hours, First Semester.

The four gospels will be studied in their relation to each other, as well as individually.   The events recorded will be brought together in one harmonious whole, each one of the Gospels making its contribution to the record of our Lord's earthly ministry.   Kerr's Harmony of the Gospel will be used.   Not **given 1918-19.**

8. Acts and Epistles.   **Two Hours, Second Semester.**

The beginning of the Christian Church as recorded in the Acts will be carefully reviewed.   The Missionary Labors of the Apostle Paul will be followed, and his epistles to the various churches established will furnish a doctrinal basis for study.   The Bible will be the principal text-book.   Not given 1918-19.

Professor Whitmer

9-10. Old Testament Literature.   Two Hours, Two Semesters.

This is a reading course covering the whole of the Old Testament in English.   It seeks to do five things: To give a knowledge of the types of literature represented in the Old Testament; to re-create the living historical background out of which the Old Testament grew; to give familiarity with the literary structure and composition of each book; to discover the point of view and purpose of each writer; to make the Bible a vital force in the life and thought of the present day.   Not **given 1918-19.**

11-12. New Testament Literature. Two Hours, Two Semesters.
The purpose of this course is to give an intimate acquaintance with the New Testament writings. Each book is considered with respect to its historical setting, literary character, author, first readers, occasion, aim and social, ethical and religious teachings.

19-20. Church History.   **Two Hours, Two Semesters.**
A general survey of the history of the Christian church from its beginnings to the present time. The topics receiving special consideration include the spread of Christianity in the Graeco-Roman world; the development of the Catholic church; the Christianization of the Teutonic peoples; the decline of the papacy; the Reformation and the development of the Protestant denominational movements, including the American church. Not given 1918-19.

Professor Langenwalter

13-14. Modern Problems in the Light of the Old Testament.
Two Hours, Two Semesters.
The question is often raised whether the Old Testament has any contribution to make to the solution of modern social and ethical problems. It is the purpose of this course to make a thorough study of those portions of the Old Testament which deal with such problems in order to find what suggestions they may contain bearing upon a possible solution of the problems of our own day.

15-16. Modern Problems in the Light of the New Testament.
Two Hours, Two Semesters.
Portions of the New Testament, dealing with social and ethical problems will be carefully investigated for the purpose of finding any suggestions they may have to offer for the solution of similar problems today as these confront the thinking man. Not given 1918-19.

18. Personal Evangelism.   **Two Hours, Second Semester.**
This course will deal with the possibilities of personal work; its limitations and the requirements for doing the same effectively and in keeping with the spirit of Christ. Not given 1918-19.

For electives, needed for the completion of the English course, see the courses offered in the Graduate Department of the Seminary.

EXPENSES

No tuition is charged in the Seminary. It is the purpose of the management to raise enough endowment to pay for the instruction as well as the other expenses.

All students pay the matriculation fee of one dollar when first entering the institution.

A library fee of two dollars per semester is the only semester fee in the Seminary.

A fee of three dollars will be charged at graduation for all students receiving degree or diploma.

Seminary students may use the Gymnasium by paying the fee of $1.50 per semester.

COURSES OFFERED IN THE MENNONITE SEMINARY

Regular Course covering three years of work, and leading to the degree of B. D.

English Course covering a period of three years. A diploma is awarded to persons completing this course.

Short Bible Courses conducted each year.

Address all communications to

The Dean of Mennonite Seminary,
Bluffton, Ohio.

REGISTER OF
ALUMNI AND STUDENTS

ALUMNI ASSOCIATION

OFFICERS

President .... A. J. Neuenschwander, '16
Vice-President .... Armin Hauenstein, '12
Secretary .... Alice Mueller, '15
Treasurer .... D. W. Bixler, '07

CLASS OF '03

Chandler, Emma Leatherman .... Dennison, Ohio
Dillman, Chas. F. .... Bluffton, Ohio
Flath, Philip .... Rockport, Ohio
Krabill, A. J. .... Wadsworth, Ohio
Lugibihl, H. R. .... Bluffton, Ohio
Owens, Joseph P. .... Toledo, Ohio
Steiner, Noah N. .... Bluffton, Ohio

CLASS OF '04

Burkholder, Florence Kohli .... Nampa, Idaho
Hilty, Dr. Oswin .... Grabill, Ind.
McPeak, Edith, Dean of Women Bluffton College...Bluffton, O.
Schumacher, Rev. Albert .... Lockwood, Ohio
Whistler, Alvin R. .... Rockport, Ohio

CLASS OF '05

Basinger, Matilda .... Chicago, Ill.
Eaton Nellie B. .... Bluffton, Ohio
Lehmann, Rosa M. .... Berne, Ind.
Lugibihl, Adah Stuckey .... Bluffton, Ohio
Wetherill, Dr. Cliff J. .... U. S. Army

CLASS OF '06

Amstutz, John Edwin, Rev. .... Halstead, Kans.
Hirschy, Caroline Ida .... Bloomington, Ind.
Hilty, C. D. .... Pandora, Ohio
Lauby, Elmer .... Bluffton, Ohio
Lehmann, G. A. .... Bluffton, Ohio
Lugibihl, M. R. .... San Antonio, N. Mex.
Schumacher, Philip .... Gary, Ind.

CLASS OF '07

Albrecht, Wm. .... Columbia, Mo.
Basinger, Ida .... New Bremen, Ohio
Burkhalter, Caroline .... Tulsa, Ariz.
Goble, Catherine Mitchell .... Findlay, Ohio
Latchaw, Lillian Egly .... Chicago, Ill.
Lugibihl, Lillian Amstutz .... San Antonio, N. Mex.
Schumacher, Cyrus .... Bluffton, Ohio
Sloan, John P. .... U. S. Army
Sommer, Selma Suter .... Crawfordsville, Iowa
Sutter, Dr. Homer A .... Ft. Oglethorpe, Ga.

CLASS OF '08

Bender, Dr. John .... Wetzel, Ohio
Chandler, Chas. .... Dennison, Ohio
Goetsch, Bertha Schifferly .... Mt. Eaton, Ohio

CLASS OF '10

Basinger, Elmer .... Bluffton, Ohio
Bixler, D. W. .... Bluffton, Ohio
Hummon, Elizabeth .... Bluffton, Ohio
Mosiman, E. E. .... Gahanna, Ohio
Mosiman, Estelle ....Middletown, Ohio
Trachsel, Chas .... Iowa City, Iowa

CLASS OF '09

McGriff, Hazel .... Bluffton, Ohio
Neuenschwander, Willis L. .... Upper Sandusky, Ohio
Sprunger, Asa .... Decatur, Ill.
Stauffer, Menno E. .... Berne, Ind.

CLASS OF '11

Steiner, Mistel Hummon ....Randolph, Ala.
Idle, Eva .... Durango, Colo.
Lehmann, Gertrude .... Clendenna, W. Va.
Luginbuhl, Della M. .... Bluffton, Ohio
Biery, Edith Morrison .... Bluffton, Ohio
Harris, Estel Whistler .... Bluffton, Ohio

CLASS OF '12

Biery, Clarence A. .... Bluffton, Ohio
Boese, T. M. .... Springfield, S. Dak.
* Burgan, Russel R. .... Carbon Hill, Ohio

oty, Inez .... Findlay, Ohio
auenstein, Armin .... U. S. Army
ennel, Bessie .... W. Middletown, Ohio
ennel, Edna .... Trenton, Ohio
ohler, Harry L. .... Celina, Ohio
antz, Effie F. .... Pulaski, Iowa
Lichty, Luella .... Pandora, Ohio
Sprunger, Helen Kennel .... Berne, Ind.
Steiner, Elvina Schumacher .... Pandora
Schumacher, Orlin .... Pandora, Ohio
Sprunger, P. P. .... Chicago, Ill.
Tschantz, Sylvia L. .... Columbus, Ohio

CLASS OF '13

Boehr, Jennie Gottshall ...... Kai Chow, Chili Province, China
Hirstein, John .... Champaign, Ill.
Mueller, Minnie .... Bluffton, Ohio
Soldner, Dora .... Berne, Ind.
Stauffer, Ruth .... Bluffton, Ohio
Temple, Eunah .... Oxford, Ohio

CLASS OF '14

Baumgartner, Martin .... Vaughnsville, Ohio
Geiger, Homer .... Bluffton, Ohio
Geiger, Luella .... Bluffton, Ohio
Henry, Mildred .... Bluffton, Ohio
Huber, Marion Clair .... Akron, Ohio
Lehmann, Metta .... Berne, Ind.
Lehmann, Caroline .... Berne, Ind.
Schlegel, Verne .... Chicago, Ill.
Sommer, Luella Hilty .... Ottawa, Ohio
Tschantz, Elrena .... Apple Creek, Ohio

CLASS OF '15

Basinger, Elmer, A. B.; B. D. .... Bluffton, Ohio
Habegger, Martha Baumgartner, A. B. .... Berne, Ind.
Crouse, May Carolus, A. B. .... Hampton, Va.
Eaton, Nellie, A. B. .... Bluffton, Ohio
Gratz, Levi, A. B. .... U. S. Army
Sprunger, Helen Kennel, A. B. .... Berne, Ind.
Martin, Nettie Moser, A. B. .... Brazil

Mueller, Alice, A. B. .... Bluffton, Ohio
Stultz, Otto, A. B. .... Van Wert, Ohio
Townsend, Charlotte, A. B. .... Harrogate, Tenn.

CLASS OF '16

Betzner, Christmas Carol, A. B. ....Ney, Ohio
Brubaker, Sarabelle, A. B. .... Leesburg, Ind.
Burkhalter, Martha Rosa, A. B. .... India
Habegger, Christine, A. B. .... Monroe, Ind.
Lehmann, Clarence O., A. B. .... West Liberty, Ohio
Luginbuhl, Della M., A. B. .... Bluffton, Ohio
Neuenschwander, Andrew J., A. B. .... Bluffton, Ohio
Rogers, Vera A., A. B. .... Hicksville, Ohio
Sommers, Selma Suter, A. B. .... Crawfordsville, Iowa
Streid, Frieda, A. B. .... Bluffton, Ohio
West, Ralph E., A. B. ....Ottumwa, Iowa

CLASS OF '17

Amstutz, Laura, A. B. .... Ft. Wayne, Ind.
Baumgartner, Martin W., A. B. .... Vaughnsville, Ohio
Habegger, Alfred, A. B., A. M. .... Berne, Ind.
Hatfield, Owen F., A. B. .... Renovo, Pa.
Kauffman, Edmund G., A. B., A. M. Kai Chow, Chili Prov., China
Kohler, Harry L., A. B. .... Celina, Ohio
Lahr, Edith, A. B. .... Black River Falls, Wisconsin
Moser, Homer, A. B. .... Armington, Ill.
Moser, Huldah, A. B. .... Sycamore, Ohio
Pannabecker, Floyd, A. B. .... Elkton, Mich.
Pannabecker, Lloyd, A. B. .... New Lexington, Ohio
Schumacher, Mary, A. B. .... Columbus Grove, Ohio
Schumacher, Waldo, A. B. .... Columbus, Ohio
Suter, Waldo, A. B. .... Wellington, Ohio
Trachsel, Charles, A. B. .... Iowa City, Iowa
Tschantz, Sylvia, A. B. .... Columbus, Ohio
Welty, Sylvan Roy, A. B. .... Princeton, N. J.

REGISTER OF STUDENTS

GRADUATE STUDENTS—1917-1918

Pannebecker, Floyd, A. B., Bluffton............Elkton, Mich.
Moyer, Samuel T., B. S. ,Bluffton..............Lansdale, Pa.

COLLEGE OF LIBERAL ARTS

COLLEGE SENIORS—1917-1918

Auten, Agnes ....Rawson, Ohio
Bixel, Mildred June .... Bluffton, Ohio
Bogart, Bernice E. .... Bluffton, Ohio
Burkhalter, Noah .... Berne, Ind.
Habegger, Metta .... Berne, Ind.
Kennel, Olga M. .... Trenton, Ohio
Krehbiel, Ruth .... Reedley, Cal.
Lehmann, Menno M. .... Drake, Sask.
Lehmann, Metta V. .... Berne, Ind.
Soldner, Dora .... Berne, Ind.
Soldner, Grover .... Berne, Ind.
Stauffer, Edwin S. .... U. S. Army
Steinman, Ethel A. .... Bluffton, Ohio
Stultz, Pauline .... Mt. Cory, Ohio
Welty, Ella .... Berne, Ind.
Welty, Paul Silas .... U. S. Army

COLLEGE JUNIORS—1917-1918

Adams, Helen .... Bluffton, Ohio
Adams, Paul .... Bluffton, Ohio
Amstutz, Omar Copeland .... Pandora, Ohio
Bauman, Harvey .... Quakertown, Pa.
Boehr, Isaac .... Henderson, Neb.
Geiger, Homer .... Bluffton, Ohio
Howe, Wilbur A. .... Hamilton, Ohio
Keiser, Austin K. .... Milford Square, Pa.
Mason, Faye .... Bluffton, Ohio
Miller, Lenore .... Ottawa, Ohio
Ramseyer, Vernon C. .... Pulaski, Iowa
Shelly, Wilmer Schantz .... U. S. Army
Stearns, Erma Leona .... Bluffton, Ohio
Strubhar, Ruth Lotta .... Washington, Ill.
Tschantz, Elrena Ethel .... Apple Creek, Ohio

COLLEGE SOPHOMORES—1917-1918

Amstutz, Agnes	Bluffton, Ohio
Amstutz, Ruth M.	Pandora, Ohio
Auten, Mary	Rawson, Ohio
Basinger, Rhoda	Pandora, Ohio
Baumgartner, Donavin A.	Bluffton, Ohio
Bixel, Gordon, A.	Bluffton, Ohio
Day, Marjorie	Bluffton, Ohio
Garber, Ella B.	Versailles, Mo.
Geiger, Beulah Lucile	Bluffton, Ohio
Geiger, Steiner F.	Bluffton, Ohio
Geiger, John	U. S. Army
Habegger, Joel	Berne, Ind.
Hochstettler, Paul E.	Bluffton, Ohio
Huber, Faery Beulah	Bluffton, Ohio
Keel, Mildred R.	Pandora, Ohio
Lahr, Cordelia H.	Bluffton, Ohio
Lahr, Marie S.	Bluffton, Ohio
Lantz, Lillian	Carlock, Ill.
Leete, Hilda	Lima, Ohio
Lehmann, Florence	Berne, Ind.
Lugibill, Estelle.Marie	Bluffton, Ohio
Montgomery, Ruth	Bluffton, Ohio
Moser, Ezra R.	Bluffton, Ohio
Myers, Aaron M.	Quakertonw, Ohio
Ringelman, Ruth Lucile	Geary, Okla.
Roth, Lelia Estella	Gibson City, Ill.
Schreyer, Glen C.	Wakarusa, Ind.
Schreyer, Raymond	Wakarusa, Ind.
Schwartzentraub, Helen	Washington, Ill.
Sprunger, Milton, F.	Berne, Ind.
Sprunger, Sybilla G.	Berne, Ind.
Stauffer, William M.	Quakertown, Pa.
Steiner, Bonnie L.	Bluffton, Ohio
Sutter, Elda Loretta	Pandora, Ohio
Thompson, J. Kimmel	Rawson, Ohio
Tschantz, Clyde M.	Dalton, Ohio
Van der Smissen, Theodore Alvin	Berne, Ind.
Welty, Delbert E.	U. S. Army
Welty, Leo D.	Apple Creek, Ohio

COLLEGE FRESHMEN—1917-1918

Adkins, Donald S. .... Lima, Ohio
Amstutz, Edith .... Bluffton, Ohio
Amstutz, Hubert M. .... Pandora, Ohio
Augsburger, Blanche .... Beaverdam, Ohio
Augsburger, Donald L. .... Bluffton, Ohio
Augspurger, Herminia .... Middletown, Ohio
Augspurger, Marie A. .... Woodburn, Ind.
Baker, Audrey .... Bluffton, Ohio
Basinger, Byron L. .... Pandora, Ohio
Basinger, Cleora .... Bluffton, Ohio
Battles, Wanda .... Bluffton, Ohio
Betzner, Genevieve .... Kitchener, Ont.
Bixel, Edna S. .... Pandora, Ohio
Bixel, Madeline .... Pandora, Ohio
Bowersox, Ina .... Rawson, Ohio
Burcky, Andrew C. .... U. S. Army
Caris, Pearl .... Bluffton, Ohio
Clymer, Fannie .... Quakertown, Pa.
Day, Allen .... Bluffton, Ohio
Farrall, Lela .... Leipsic, Ohio
Franz, Gerhard .... Berne, Ind.
Freed, Leigh B. .... Williamstown, Ohio
Gerber, Leona .... Pandora, Ohio
Gratz, Cora .... Bluffton, Ohio
Gratz, Elizabeth .... Bluffton, Ohio
Gratz, Lillie .... Bluffton, Ohio
Gottshall, Herbert .... Bluffton, Ohio
Habegger, Bulinna .... Pandora, Ohio
Hall, Doyt P. .... Lafayette, Ohio
Hammack, Pauline .... Lima, Ohio
Hawk, Mabel .... Bluffton, Ohio
Hecathorne, Chloe .... Rawson, Ohio
Heller, Mae .... Pittsburg, Pa.
Herr, Rowena .... Bluffton, Ohio
Hilty, Gertrude .... Pandora, Ohio
Hower, Pauline .... Rawson, Ohio
Huffman, Irene .... New Carlisle, Ohio
Jantz, Jacob G. .... Drake, Sask.

Johns, Nina .... Pandora, Ohio
Kidd, Mamie .... Bluffton, Ohio
Koch, Albert .... U. S. Army
Kohli, Martha .... Pandora, Ohio
Lehman, Inez .... Pandora, Ohio
Lehmann, Menno .... Berne, Ind.
Loganbill, Orvilla .... Geary, Okla.
Lugibill, Esta .... Bluffton, Ohio
McKee, Lucile .... Beaverdam, Ohio
McKinley, Opal .... Bluffton, Ohio
Moser, Elizabeth .... Bluffton, Ohio
Neuenschwander, Marie .... Bluffton, Ohio
Oen, Cora M. .... Lima, Ohio
Owens, Frances .... Bluffton, Ohio
Rediger, Joseph .... Meadows, Ill.
Rickert, Abram .... Souderton, Pa.
Rogers, Roy .... Bluffton, Ohio
Roth, Freeda .... Gibson City, Ill.
Rudy, Ruth .... Bluffton, Ohio
Rupp, Blanche .... Bluffton, Ohio
Scheid, Harriet .... Bluffton, Ohio
Scheid, Theo. G. .... Bluffton, Ohio
Schmitt, Marguerite .... Moundridge, Kansas
Schumacher, Oliver .... Pandora, Ohio
Schutz, Huldah .... Pandora, Ohio
Stearns, Mamie .... Bluffton, Ohio
Steiner, Elizabeth .... Pandora, Ohio
Steider, Freda .... Meadows, Ill.
Steiner, Geneva .... Bluffton, Ohio
Steiner, Irma C. .... Pandora, Ohio
Stettler, Clair .... Bluffton, Ohio
Strow, Kahtoma .... Columbus Grove, Ohio
Studer, Clair W. .... Apple Creek, Ohio
Triplehorn, Edith .... Bluffton, Ohio
Urich, Louise .... Lafayette, Ohio
Welty, Fred .... U. S. Army
Wenger, Harry .... Wayland, Iowa
Wulliman, Raymond C. .... Berne, Ind.

COLLEGE SPECIAL

Boothby, Ilo J. .... Bluffton, Ohio
Cunningham, Dae .... Arlington, Ohio
Hilty, Verena .... Bluffton, Ohio
Mason, Bertha .... Bluffton, Ohio
Roethlisberger, Bertha .... Bluffton, Ohio

PREPARATORY

Amstutz, Rhoda .... Bluffton, Ohio
Anderson, Alvin A. .... U. S. Army
Ewing, Geraldine .... Bluffton, Ohio
Flueckiger, Samuel .... Berne, Ind.
Good, Adah .... Bluffton, Ohio
Guth, Harold L. .... Washington, Ill.
Roethlisberger, Selma .... Bluffton, Ohio
Sprunger, Rose .... Berne, Ind.
Steinman, Edna .... Carlock, Ill.
Stutzman, Joash H. .... Carlock, Ill.
Yoder, Florence .... Bluffton, Ohio
Zuercher, Oswin E. .... Berne, Ind.
Zuercher, Jephtha W. .... Berne, Ind.

SHORT AGRICULTURE COURSE

Althaus, William .... Bluffton, Ohio
Bixel, Truman .... Bluffton, Ohio
Hilty, Melvin S. .... Beaverdam, Ohio
King, Leonard E. .... Carlock, Ill.
Miller, Milo Allen .... Pekin, Ill.

MENNONITE SEMINARY

GRADUATE COURSE

Basinger, Elmer A. B., B. D., Bluffton..........Bluffton, Ohio
Bechtel, Andrew. S.,A. B. Buchnell,..............Bluffton, Ohio
Moyer, John F., A. B. Bethel ....Pandora, Ohio
Moyer, Samuel T., B. S., Penn State,...........Lansdale, Pa.
Neuenschwander, Andrew J., A. B., Bluffton....Bluffton, Ohio
Pannebecker, Floyd, A. B., Bluffton...........Elkton, Mich.
Soldner, Grover .... Berne, Ind.

ENGLISH COURSE

Lester H. Bixel .... Bluffton, Ohio
Esch, Benjamin F. .... Bluffton, Ohio
Esch, Anna E. .... Bluffton, Ohio
Hallman, Bertie .... Kitchener, Ont.
Lambert, Norah M. .... Elkhart, Ind.
Marker, Mae ....New Madison, Ohio
Mitchell, Leroy .... Lima, Ohio
Neuenschwander, Mrs. A. J. .... Bluffton, Ohio
Schutt Ruth A. ....South Bend, Ind.

SHORT BIBLE COURSE

Badertscher, Elma .... Dalton, Ohio
Beck, Ottilia M. .... Carlock, Ill.
Bixel, Edna S. .... Pandora, Ohio
Boehr, John .... Wisner, Nebr.
Boehr, Lena .... Wisner, Nebr.
Deppler, J. C. .... Bluffton, Ohio
Grismore, Elizabeth .... Bluffton, Ohio
Herman, Allen .... Windermere, Ohio
Huffman, Russell J. .... New Carlisle, Ohio
Kennel, Ralph .... Middletown, Ohio
Leatherman, Priscilla .... Milford Square, Pa.
Niswander, Eunice .... Beaverdam, Ohio
Rediger, Mrs. C. E. .... Bluffton, Ohio
Schumacher, Florence .... Bluffton, Ohio
Steiner, Irma C. .... Pandora, Ohio
Welty, Mary S. .... Pandora, Ohio

CONSERVATORY OF MUSIC

Adams, Helen, ... Bluffton, Ohio
Adams, Paul A. .... Bluffton, Ohio
Adkins, Donald S. .... Lima, Ohio
Althaus, Hallie .... Bluffton, Ohio
Amstutz, Marie .... Bluffton, Ohio
Amstutz, May Ola .... Bluffton, Ohio
Amstutz, R. Mendelssohn .... Pandora, Ohio
Amstutz, Omar C. .... Pandora, Ohio
Amstutz, Rhoda .... Bluffton, Ohio
Badertscher, Elma ....Dalton, Ohio
Baker, Emmett .... Rawson, Ohio

Basinger, Lester, ... Pandora, Ohio
Baumgartner, Magdalene, ... Bluffton, Ohio
Baker, Andrey .... Bluffton, Ohio
Basinger, Cleora .... Bluffton, Ohio
Basinger, Garland .... Bluffton, Ohio
Beeshy, Glenna .... Bluffton, Ohio
Berkey, Herbert W. .... Bluffton, Ohio
Beeshy, Vivian .... Bluffton, Ohio
Betzner, Genevieve .... Kitchener, Ont.
Biederman, Rosella .... Bluffton, Ohio
Biery, Edith Morrison .... Bluffton, Ohio
Bixel, Edna .... Pandora, Ohio
Bixel, Clara .... Bluffton, Ohio
Boehr, John .... Wisner, Nebraska
Boehr, Lena .... Wisner, Nebraska
Bogart, Bernice .... Bluffton, Ohio
Bogart, Harold .... Bluffton, Ohio
Bogart, Eddyth .... Bluffton, Ohio
Bowersox, Ina .... Rawson, Ohio
Bracy, Hannah .... Bluffton, Ohio
Bracy, Jesse .... Bluffton, Ohio
Burkholder, Ella M. .... Bluffton, Ohio
Burkholder, Lavina J. .... Bluffton, Ohio
Burkhalter, Noah ....Berne, Ind.
Burcky, Andrew C. ....Tiskilwa, Ill.
Burkholder, Rhoda E. .... Bluffton, Ohio
Byers, Robert .... Bluffton, Ohio
Byers, Floyd .... Bluffton, Ohio
Caris, Pearl .... Ada, Ohio
Crosser, Ruth .... Bluffton, Ohio
Ewing, Geraldine .... Bluffton, Ohio
Fett, Ellen .... Bluffton, Ohio
Franz, Elfrieda .... Berne, Ind.
Franz, Gerhard .... Berne, Ind.
Flueckiger, Samuel .... Berne, Ind.
Freed, Leigh B. .... Williamstown, Ohio
Garber, Leona I. .... Pandora, Ohio
Warwood, Merwin .... Williamstown, Ohio
Geiger, Steiner F. .... Bluffton, Ohio

Geiger, Lillian .... Bluffton, Ohio
Gratz, Cora .... Bluffton, Ohio
Good, Adah .... Bluffton, Ohio
Goebel, Mildred .... Bluffton, Ohio
Gottshall Herbert .... Bluffton, Ohio
Gratz, Elizabeth .... Bluffton, Ohio
Guth, Harold .... Washington, Ill.
Grismore, Elizabeth .... Bluffton, Ohio
Habegger, Bulinna .... Pandora, Ohio
Habegger, Ella .... Berne, Ind.
Habegger, Joel F. .... Berne, Ind.
Hallman, Bertie .... Kitchener, Ont.
Hammack, Pauline E. .... Lima, Ohio
Harris, Mabel .... Mt. Cory, Ohio
Hawk, Mabel .... Bluffton, Ohio
Hauenstein, Kent .... Bluffton, Ohio
Hecathorne, Chloe .... Rawson, Ohio
Heller, S. Mae .... Pittsburg, Pa.
Herr, Rowena .... Bluffton, Ohio
Herman, Allen .... Windermere, Ohio
Hiestand, Geneva .... Chapel, Pa.
Hilty, Gertrude .... Pandora, Ohio
Hower, Pauline .... Rawson, Ohio
Huffman, Irene .... New Carlisle, Ohio
Huffman, Paul .... Bluffton, Ohio
Huffman, Russel .... Carlisle, Ohio
Huber, Faery .... Bluffton, Ohio
Hughson, Robert .... Bluffton, Ohio
Jantz, Jacob G. .... Drake, Sask.
Jones, Ora .... Bluffton, Ohio
Johns, Nina M. .... Pandora, Ohio
Kennel, Olga M. .... Trenton, Ohio
Kidd, Mamie .... Bluffton, Ohio
Kohler, Lydia .... Bluffton, Ohio
Kohli, Martha .... Pandora, Ohio
Klay, Eva .... Bluffton ,Ohio
Krehbiel, Ruth .... Reedley, Calif.
Leatherman, Priscilla .... Quakertown, Pa.
Lehmann, Florence .... Berne, Ind.

Lehmann, Inez .... Pandora, Ohio
Lehmann, Menno .... Berne, Ind.
Locher, Ruth .... Bluffton, Ohio
Loganbill, Orvilla .... Geary, Okla.
Lora, Helen .... Bluffton, Ohio
Luginbuhl, Della .... Bluffton, Ohio
Lugibill, Estelle .... Bluffton, Ohio
Lugibill, Kathleen .... Bluffton, Ohio
Lugibihl, Salome .... Bluffton, Ohio
McKillip, Maxine .... Columbus Grove, Ohio
McKinley, Opal .... Bluffton, Ohio
Moser, Hallie M. .... Pandora, Ohio
Myers, Gretta .... Bluffton, Ohio
Neuenschwander, Eunice .... Beaverdam, Ohio
Owens, Frances .... Bluffton, Ohio
Reiter, Bliss Ara .... Mt. Cory, Ohio
Ringelman, Ruth .... Geary, Okla.
Roth, Freeda .... Gibson City, Ill.
Roth, Lelia E. .... Gibson City, Ill.
Rudy, Harry .... Bluffton, Ohio
Rudy, Ruth .... Bluffton, Ohio
Rupp, Blanche .... Beaverdam, Ohio
Schmidt, Margaret .... Moundridge, Kan.
Schryer, Glenn .... Wakarusa, Ind.
Schumacher, Florence .... Bluffton, Ohio
Scoles, Glen .... Bluffton, Ohio
Schryer, Raymond R. .... Wakarusa, Ind.
Schumacher, Clara .... Pandora, Ohio
Schumacher, Oliver .... Pandora, Ohio
Schutz, Hulda .... Pandora, Ohio
Scoles, Nelle .... Bluffton, Ohio
Soldner, Grover .... Berne, Ind.
Smith, Earl .... Rawson, Ohio
Smith, Paul .... Rawson, Ohio
Sprunger, Sybilla .... Berne, Ind.
Sprunger, Milton F. .... Berne, Ind.
Stauffer, William .... Quakertown, Pa.
Stearns, Erma L. .... Bluffton, Ohio
Stearns, Mamie .... Bluffton, Ohio

Steiner, Bonnie .... Bluffton, Ohio
Steiner, Elizabeth .... Pandora, Ohio
Steiner, Clorinda .... Bluffton ,Ohio
Steiner, Geneva .... Bluffton, Ohio
Steiner, Irma............................... Bluffton, Ohio
Steiner, Margaret .... Bluffton ,Ohio
Steinman, Ethel .... Bluffton, Ohio
Steinman, Edna .... Carlock, Ill.
Stettler, Clair .... Bluffton, Ohio
Strubhar, Ruth, ...Washington, Ill.
Studer, Clair .... Apple Creek, Ohio
Sutter, Carrie ....Bluffton, Ohio
Sutter, Elda, ... Toledo, Ohio
Sutter, Elvira .... Bluffton, Ohio
Sumney, Wilbur .... Bluffton, Ohio
Thompson, Violetta .... Bluffton, Ohio
Thut, Bernice .... Beaverdam, Ohio
Thompson, J. Kimmel .... Rawson, Ohio
Thierstein, L. Wallace .... Bluffton, Ohio
Triplehorn, Edith .... Bluffton, Ohio
Tschantz, Clyde .... Dalton, Ohio
Urich, Louise .... LaFayette, Ohio
Wagner, Aura R. .... Mt. Cory, Ohio
Watkins, Evelyn .... Bluffton, Ohio
Welty, Ella .... Berne, Ind.
Welty, Paul Silas .... Ft. Wayne, Ind.
Wenger, Harry .... Wayland, Iowa
Williams, Naoma .... Bluffton, Ohio
Woods, Mrs. S. K. .... Rawson, Ohio
Wulliman, Raymond .... Berne, Ind.
Yentz, Grace Murray .... Bluffton, Ohio
Zehrbach, Edgar .... Bluffton, Ohio
Zimmerly, Elizabeth .... Bluffton, Ohio

SUMMER SCHOOL 1917-1918

Adams, Edith Mae .... Lima, Ohio
Allgyer, Ruth E. .... West Liberty, Ohio
Amstutz, Marie .... Bluffton, Ohio
Baker, Emmit M. .... Rawson, Ohio
Bash, Edwin W. .... Zanesville, Ohio

Biedermann, Rosella Louise .... Bluffton, Ohio
Bixel, Mildred, J. .... Bluffton, Ohio
Block, Robert A. .... Lima, Ohio
Bogart, Bernice .... Bluffton, Ohio
Bogart, Eddyth .... Bluffton, Ohio
Boyer, Ulalah .... Spencerville, Ohio
Bracy, Hannah .... Bluffton, Ohio
Brown, Hazel Ruth .... West Minster, Ohio
Burkholder, Ella .... Bluffton, Ohio
Burkholder, Lavina .... Bluffton, Ohio
Burkholder, Rhoda .... Bluffton, Ohio
Campbell, Flossie .... Quincy, Ohio
Criblez, Rachel .... Beaverdam, Ohio
Cunningham, Dae .... Arlington, Ohio
Day, Marjorie .... Bluffton, Ohio
Davidson, Reno .... Bluffton, Ohio
Davis, Cecil .... Bluffton, Ohio
Deeds, Dwight .... Bluffton, Ohio
Ewing, Geraldine .... Bluffton, Ohio
Fett, Clara .... Bluffton, Ohio
Flick, Ferne Vivian .... Bluffton, Ohio
Folk, Ruth .... Mt. Cory, Ohio
Franz, Elfrieda .... Berne, Ind.
Funk, Tina .... Sask.
Geiger, Luella .... Bluffton, Ohio
Goble, Mildred .... Beaverdam, Ohio
Good, Adah .... Bluffton, Ohio
Gratz, Marie Elizabeth .... Bluffton, Ohio
Grothaus, Chas. R. .... New Bremen, Ohio
Habegger, Joe F. .... Berne, Ind.
Habegger, Metta .... Berne, Ind.
Headings, Ada .... West Liberty, Ohio
Hiestand, Geneva K. .... Chapel, Pa.
Hilty, Verena .... Bluffton, Ohio
Hochstettler, Paul .... Bluffton, Ohio
Hootman, Ardis .... Hicksville, Ohio
Hughson, Robert .... Bluffton, Ohio
Kauffman, Kennion K. .... Bremen, Ind.
Kennel, Edna .... Trenton, Ohio

Kennel, Olga M. .... Trenton, Ohio
King, W. S. .... Mt. Cory, Ohio
Klay, Eva .... Bluffton, Ohio
Kohli, Hiram M. .... Pandora, Ohio
Kohli, Homer J. .... U. S. Army
Koontz, Ruth .... Bluffton, Ohio
Kuck, Clara .... New Knoxville, Ohio
Lahr, Edith .... Bluffton, Ohio
Lambert, Florence .... Lima, Ohio
Lehman, Caroline .... Berne, Ind.
Lowry, Gwendolin .... Bluffton, Ohio
Loy, Mae .... McComb, Ohio
Lugibill, Estelle .... Bluffton, Ohio
Lugibill, Kathleen .... Bluffton, Ohio
Mason, Fay .... Bluffton, Ohio
Mason, Naomi .... Bluffton, Ohio
McCollough, Beulah .... Hicksville, Ohio
McKee, Lucille .... Beaverdam, Ohio
McPherron, Doyle .... Lima, Ohio
Miller, Merle .... Bluffton, Ohio
Montgomery, Ruth .... Bluffton, Ohio
Moser, Hallie M. .... Bluffton, Ohio
Murray, Ruth .... Bluffton, Ohio
Newson, Elizabeth .... Lima, Ohio
Owens, Sarah .... Bluffton, Ohio
Otis, Elizabeth .... Hicksville, Ohio
Plaugher, Lee Roy .... Beaverdam, Ohio
Rediger, Joseph .... Meadows, Ill.
Riffel, Orvill .... Greenville, Ohio
Roeder, Edith .... Lima, Ohio
Rudy, Ruth .... Bluffton, Ohio
Schumacher, Clara .... Bluffton, Ohio
Schumacher, Florence .... Bluffton, Ohio
Schryer, Raymond R. .... Wakarusa, Ind.
Shelly, Wilmer S. .... U. S. Army
Shrider, Vance S. .... U. S. Army
Smith, Earl E. .... Rawson, Ohio
Smith, Lseter B. .... Berne, Ind.
Smith, Paul C. .... Bluffton, Ohio

Soldner, Grover T. .... Berne, Ind.
Soldner, Zilla .... Berne, Ind.
Sommers, Edwin .... Beaverdam, Ohio
Sommers, Josephine .... Crawfordsville, Ohio
Sprunger, Clifton .... Berne, Ind.
Steiner, Bonnie .... Bluffton, Ohio
Steiner, Edith ....Bluffton, Ohio
Steiner, Naoma .... Bluffton, Ohio
Steiner, Marie .... Bluffton, Ohio
Steiner, Mildred .... Bluffton, Ohio
Steinman, Ethel .... Bluffton, Ohio
Stoodt, Dae .... Beaverdam, Ohio
Stratton, Mildred .... Bluffton, Ohio
Stultz, Pauline L. .... Mt. Cory, Ohio
Sutter, Elda .... Toledo, Ohio
Sutter, Elvira .... Bluffton, Ohio
Thut, Pearl .... Lima, Ohio
Valet, Rosa C. .... Edgerton, Ohio
Woods, Lillian .... Bluffton, Ohio
Wright, Lucile ....·...................... Spencerville, Ohio
Yoder, Florence Christine .... Bluffton, Ohio
Zerbst, Florence Louise ..·.................. Lima, Ohio

SUMMARY BY DEPARTMENTS

College of Liberal Arts 153
Preparatory Department 13
Short Agriculture Course 5
Seminary 16
Short Bible Course 16
Conservatory 161
Summer School 105

                         Total   468
Net total counting each but once 340

SUMMARY BY STATES

Canada 4
California 2
Indiana 27
Illinois 13
Iowa 2
Kansas 1
Michigan 1
Missouri 1
Nebraska 3
Ohio 258
Oklahoma 2
Pennsylvania 11
W. Virginia 1
U. S. Army 14

INDEX

Lightning Source UK Ltd.
Milton Keynes UK
UKHW041633040119
334726UK00010B/1076/P